KARL MARX

THE CIVIL WAR IN FRANCE

With an introduction by

FREDERICK ENGELS

INTERNATIONAL PUBLISHERS

NEW YORK

CONTENTS

EDITOR'S NOTE

Most of the previous editions of *The Civil War in France* contained only the main Address presented by Karl Marx to the General Council of the First International on May 30th, 1871, two days after the fall of the Paris Commune. When these editions included the two earlier Addresses, which dealt with the Franco-Prussian War, they were usually used as appendices to the volume.

As Engels suggests in his introduction written on the twentieth anniversary of the Commune, the two shorter Addresses, also written by Marx, should be included ahead of the celebrated Address which drew the classic lessons of the rise and fall of the Commune. This is done in this edition.

In two letters to his friend Dr. Kugelmann, Marx wrote on April 12th and 17th, 1871, making several significant observations regarding the Commune. Excerpts from these letters, praised highly by Lenin, are included in this volume.

The reference and explanatory notes at the end of the volume deal not only with names, events, dates, places, etc., but also contain numerous excerpts from the writings of Lenin on the Commune which was always to him both a source of study and inspiration. When the Socialist Revolution in Russia established the Soviet Commune, Lenin paid high tribute to the first Commune when he declared that the young Soviet Republic stood on the shoulders of the Paris Commune.

THE CIVIL WAR IN FRANCE

Introduction by Frederick Engels

I DID not anticipate that I would be asked to prepare a new edition of the Address of the General Council of the International on *The Civil War in France,* and to write an introduction to it. Therefore I can only touch briefly here on the most important points.

I am prefacing the longer work mentioned above by the two shorter Addresses of the General Council on the Franco-Prussian War. In the first place, because the second of these, which itself cannot be fully understood without the first, is referred to in *The Civil War.* But also because these two Addresses, likewise drafted by Marx, are, no less than *The Civil War,* outstanding examples of the author's remarkable gift, first proved in *The Eighteenth Brumaire of Louis Bonaparte,* for grasping clearly the character, the import, and the necessary consequences of great historical events, at a time when these events are still in process before our eyes, or have only just taken place. And, finally, because we in Germany are still having to endure the consequences which Marx prophesied would follow from these events.

Has that which was declared in the first Address not come to pass: that if Germany's defensive war against Louis Bonaparte degenerated into a war of conquest against the French people, all the misfortunes which befell Germany after the so-called wars of liberation [1] would revive again with renewed intensity? Have we not had a further twenty years of Bismarck's government, the Exceptional Law and the anti-socialist campaign taking the place of the prosecutions of "demagogues," with the same arbitrary police measures and with literally the same staggering interpretations of the law?

And has not the prophecy been proved to the letter that the

9

annexation of Alsace-Lorraine would "force France into the arms of Russia,"[2] and that after this annexation Germany must either become the avowed tool of Russia, or must, after some short respite, arm for a new war, and, moreover, "a war with the combined Slavonian and Roman races"? Has not the annexation of the French provinces driven France into the arms of Russia? Has not Bismarck for fully twenty years vainly wooed the favour of the tsar, wooed it with services even more lowly than those which little Prussia, before it became the "first Power in Europe," was wont to lay at Holy Russia's feet? And is there not every day hanging over our heads the Damocles' sword of war, on the first day of which all the chartered covenants of princes will be scattered like chaff; a war of which nothing is certain but the absolute uncertainty of its outcome; a race war which will subject the whole of Europe to devastation by fifteen or twenty million armed men, and is only not already raging because even the strongest of the great military states shrinks before the absolute incalculability of its final outcome?

All the more is it our duty to make again accessible to the German workers these brilliant proofs, now half-forgotten, of the far-sightedness of international working class policy in 1870.

What is true of these two Addresses is also true of *The Civil War in France*. On May 28, the last fighters of the Commune succumbed to superior forces on the slopes of Belleville; and only two days later, on May 30, Marx read to the General Council the work in which the historical significance of the Paris Commune is delineated in short powerful strokes, but with such clearness, and above all such truth, as has never again been attained in all the mass of literature which has been written on this subject.

Thanks to the economic and political development of France since 1789, for fifty years the position in Paris has been such that no revolution could break out there without assuming a proletarian character, that is to say, without the proletariat, which had bought victory with its blood, advancing its own demands after victory. These demands were more or less unclear and even confused, corresponding to the state of evolution reached by the workers of Paris at the particular period, but in the last resort they all amounted to the abolition of the class antagonism between capitalists and workers. It is true that no one knew how this was to be brought about. But the demand itself, however indefinite it still was in its formulation, contained a threat to the existing order of society; the workers who put it forward were still armed; therefore the disarming of the workers was the first commandment for the bourgeois at the helm of the state. Hence, after every revolution won by the workers, a new struggle, ending with the defeat of the workers.

This happened for the first time in 1848. The liberal bourgeoisie of the parliamentary opposition held banquets for securing reform of the franchise, which was to ensure supremacy for their party. Forced more and more, in their struggle with the government, to appeal to the people, they had to allow the radical and republican strata of the bourgeoisie and petty bourgeoisie gradually to take the lead. But behind these stood the revolutionary workers, and since 1830 these had acquired far more political independence than the bourgeoisie, and even the republicans, suspected. At the moment of the crisis between the government and the opposition, the workers opened battle on the streets; Louis Philippe vanished, and with him the franchise reform; and in its place arose the republic, and indeed one which the victorious workers themselves designated as a "social" republic. No one, however, was clear as to what this social republic was to imply; not even the workers themselves. But they now had arms in their hands, and were a power in the state. Therefore, as soon as the bourgeois republicans in control felt something like firm ground under their feet, their first aim was to disarm the workers. This took place by driving them into the insurrection of June 1848 by direct breach of faith, by open defiance and the attempt to banish the unemployed to a distant province. The government had taken care to have an overwhelming superiority of force. After five days' heroic struggle, the workers were defeated. And then followed a blood-bath of the defenceless prisoners, the like of which has not been seen since the days of the civil wars which ushered in the downfall of the Roman republic. It was the first time that the bourgeoisie showed to what insane cruelties of revenge they will be goaded the moment the proletariat dares to take its stand against them as a separate class, with its own interests and demands. And yet 1848 was only child's play compared with their frenzy in 1871.

Punishment followed hard at heel. If the proletariat was not yet able to rule France, the bourgeoisie could no longer do so. At least not at that period, when the greater part of it was still monarchically inclined, and it was divided into three dynastic parties [3] and a fourth republican party. Its internal dissensions allowed the adventurer Louis Bonaparte to take possession of all the commanding points—army, police, administrative machinery—and, on December 2, 1851,[4] to explode the last stronghold of the bourgeoisie, the National Assembly. The Second Empire [5] opened the exploitation of France by a gang of political and financial adventurers, but at the same time also an industrial development such as had never been possible under the narrow-minded and timorous system of Louis Philippe, with its exclusive domination by only a small section of the big bourgeoisie. Louis Bonaparte took the political power from the capitalists under the pretext of protecting them, the bourgeoisie, from the workers, and on the other hand the workers from them; but in return his rule encouraged speculation and industrial activity—in a word the rise and enrichment of the whole bourgeoisie to an extent hitherto unknown. To an even greater extent, it is true, corruption and mass robbery developed, clustering around the imperial court, and drawing their heavy percentages from this enrichment.

But the Second Empire was the appeal to French chauvinism, the demand for the restoration of the frontiers of the First Empire, which had been lost in 1814, or at least those of the First Republic. A French empire within the frontiers of the old monarchy and, in fact, within the even more amputated frontiers of 1815—such a thing was impossible for any long duration of time. Hence the necessity for brief wars and extension of frontiers. But no extension of frontiers was so dazzling to the imagination of the French chauvinists as the extension to the German left bank of the Rhine. One square mile on the Rhine was more to them than ten in the Alps or anywhere else. Given the Second Empire, the demand for the restoration to France of the left bank of the Rhine, either all at once or piecemeal, was merely a question of time. The time came with the Austro-Prussian War of 1866; [6] cheated of the anticipated "territorial compensation" by Bismarck and by his own over-cunning, hesitating policy, there was now nothing left for Napoleon but war, which broke out in 1870 and drove him first to Sedan, [7] and thence to Wilhelmshöhe.

The inevitable result was the Paris Revolution of September 4, 1870. The empire collapsed like a house of cards, and the republic was again proclaimed. But the enemy was standing at the gates; the armies of the empire were either hopelessly beleaguered in Metz or held captive in Germany. In this emergency the people allowed the Paris deputies to the former legislative body to constitute themselves into a "Government of National Defence." This was the more readily conceded, since, for the purposes of defence, all Parisians capable of bearing arms had enrolled in the National Guard and were armed, so that now the workers constituted a great majority. But almost at once the antagonism between the almost completely bourgeois government and the armed proletariat broke into open conflict. On October 31, workers' battalions stormed the town hall, and captured some members of the government. Treachery, the government's direct breach of its undertakings, and the intervention of some petty-bourgeois battalions set them free again, and in order not to occasion the outbreak of civil war inside a city which was already beleaguered by a foreign power, the former government was left in office.

At last, on January 8, 1871, Paris, almost starving, capitulated but with honours unprecedented in the history of war. The forts were surrendered, the outer wall disarmed, the weapons of the regiments of the line and of the Mobile Guard [8] were handed over, and they themselves considered prisoners of war. But the National Guard kept its weapons and guns, and only entered into an armistice with the victors, who themselves did not dare enter Paris in triumph. They only dared to occupy a tiny corner of Paris, which, into the bargain, consisted partly of public parks, and even this they only occupied for a few days! And during this time they, who had maintained their encirclement of Paris for 131 days, were themselves encircled by the armed workers of Paris, who kept a sharp watch that no "Prussian" should overstep the narrow bounds of the corner ceded to the foreign conquerors. Such was the respect which the Paris workers inspired in the army before which all the armies of the empire had laid down their arms; and the Prussian *Junkers,* who had come to take revenge at the very centre of the revolution, were compelled to stand by respectfully, and salute just precisely this armed revolution!

During the war the Paris workers had confined themselves to demanding the vigorous prosecution of the fight. But now, when peace had come after the capitulation of Paris, now, Thiers, the new head of the government, was compelled to realise that the supremacy of the propertied classes—large landowners and capitalists—was in constant danger so long as the workers of Paris had arms in their hands. His first action was to attempt to disarm them. On March 18, he sent troops of the line with orders to rob the National Guard of the artillery belonging to it, which had been constructed during the siege of Paris and had been paid for by subscription. The attempt failed; Paris mobilised as one man in defence of the guns, and war between Paris and the French government sitting at Versailles was declared. On March 26 the Paris Commune was elected and on March 28 it was proclaimed. The Central Committee of the National Guard, which up to then had carried on the government, handed in its resignation to the National Guard, after it had first decreed the abolition of the scandalous Paris "Morality Police." On March 30 the Commune abolished conscription and the standing army, and declared that the National Guard, in which all citizens capable of bearing arms were to be enrolled, was to be the sole armed force. It remitted all payments of rent for dwelling houses from October 1870 until April, the amounts already paid to be reckoned to a future rental period, and stopped all sales of articles pledged in the municipal pawnshops. On the same day the foreigners elected to the Commune were confirmed in office, because "the flag of the Commune is the flag of the World Republic."

On April 1 it was decided that the highest salary received by any employee of the Commune, and therefore also by its members themselves, might not exceed 6,000 francs. On the following day the Commune decreed the separation of the Church from the State, and the abolition of all state payments for religious purposes as well as the transformation of all Church property into national property; as a result of which, on April 8, a decree excluding from the schools all religious symbols, pictures, dogmas, prayers—in a word, "all that belongs to the sphere of the individual's conscience" —was ordered to be excluded from the schools, and this decree was gradually applied. On the 5th, in reply to the shooting, day after day, of the Commune's fighters captured by the Versailles troops, a decree was issued for imprisonment of hostages, but it was never carried into effect. On the 6th, the guillotine was brought out by the 137th battalion of the National Guard, and publicly burnt, amid great popular rejoicing. On the 12th, the Commune decided that the Victory Column on the Place Vendôme, which had been cast from guns captured by Napoleon after the war of 1809, should be demolished as a symbol of chauvinism and incitement to national hatred. This decree was carried out on May 16. On April 16 the Commune ordered a statistical tabulation of factories which had been closed down by the manufacturers, and the working out of plans for the carrying on of these factories by workers formerly employed in them, who were to be organised in co-operative societies, and also plans for the organisation of these co-operatives in one great union. On the 20th the Commune abolished night work for bakers, and also the workers' registration cards, which since the Second Empire had been run as a monopoly by police nominees— exploiters of the first rank; the issuing of these registration cards was transferred to the mayors[9] of the twenty *arrondissements* of Paris. On April 30 the Commune ordered the closing of the pawn-shops, on the ground that they were a private exploitation of labour, and were in contradiction with the right of the workers to their instruments of labour and to credit. On May 5 it ordered the demolition of the Chapel of Atonement, which had been built in expiation of the execution of Louis XVI.[10]

Thus, from March 18 onwards the class character of the Paris movement, which had previously been pushed into the background by the fight against the foreign invaders, emerged sharply and clearly. As almost without exception, workers, or recognised representatives of the workers, sat in the Commune, its decisions bore a decidedly proletarian character. Either they decreed reforms which the republican bourgeoisie had failed to pass solely out of cowardice, but which provided a necessary basis for the free activity of the working class—such as the realisation of the principle that *in relation to the state,* religion is a purely private matter—or they promulgated decrees which were in the direct interests of the working class and to some extent cut deeply into the old order of society. In a beleaguered city, however, it was possible at most to make a start in the realisation of all these measures. And from the beginning of May onwards all their energies were taken up by the fight against the ever-growing armies assembled by the Versailles government.

On April 7 the Versailles troops had captured the Seine crossing at Neuilly, on the western front of Paris; on the other hand, in an attack on the southern front on the 11th they were repulsed with heavy losses by General Eudes. Paris was continually bombarded and, moreover, by the very people who had stigmatised as a sacrilege the bombardment of the same city by the Prussians. These same people now begged the Prussian government for the hasty return of the French soldiers taken prisoner at Sedan and Metz, in order that they might recapture Paris for them. From the beginning of May the gradual arrival of these troops gave the Versailles forces a decided ascendancy. This already became evident when, on April 23, Thiers broke off the negotiations for the exchange, proposed by the Commune, of the Archbishop of Paris and a whole number of other priests held as hostages in Paris, for only one man, Blanqui, who had twice been elected to the Commune but was a prisoner in Clairvaux. And even more in the changed language of Thiers; previously procrastinating and equivocal, he now suddenly became insolent, threatening, brutal. The Versailles forces took the redoubt of Moulin Saquet on the southern front, on May 3; on the 9th, Fort Issy, which had been completely reduced to ruins by gunfire; and on the 14th, Fort Vanves. On the western front they advanced gradually, capturing the numerous villages and buildings which extended up to the city wall, until they reached the main wall itself; on the 21st, thanks to treachery and the carelessness of the National Guards stationed there, they succeeded in forcing their way into the city. The Prussians who held the northern and eastern forts allowed the Versailles troops to advance across the land north of the city, which was forbidden ground to them under the armistice, and thus to march forward and attack on a long front, which the Parisians naturally thought covered by the armistice, and therefore held only with weak forces. As a result of this, only a weak resistance was put up in the western half of Paris, in the luxury city proper; it grew stronger and more tenacious the nearer the incoming troops approached the eastern half, the real working class city.

It was only after eight days' fighting that the last defenders of the Commune were overwhelmed on the heights of Belleville and Menilmontant; and then the massacre of defenceless men, women and children, which had been raging all through the week on an increasing scale, reached its zenith. The breechloaders could no longer kill fast enough; the vanquished workers were shot down in hundreds by mitrailleuse fire. The "Wall of the Federals" at the Père Lachaise cemetery, where the final mass murder was consummated, is still standing today, a mute but eloquent testimony to the savagery of which the ruling class is capable as soon as the working class dares to come out for its rights. Then came the mass arrests; when the slaughter of them all proved to be impossible, the shooting of victims arbitrarily selected from the prisoners' ranks, and the removal of the rest to great camps where they awaited trial by courts-martial. The Prussian troops surrounding the northern half of Paris had orders not to allow any fugitives to pass; but the officers often shut their eyes when the soldiers paid more obedience to the dictates of humanity than to those of the General Staff; particularly, honour is due to the Saxon army corps, which behaved very humanely and let through many workers who were obviously fighters for the Commune.

If today, after twenty years, we look back at the activity and historical significance of the Paris Commune of 1871, we shall find it necessary to make a few additions to the account given in *The Civil War in France.*

The members of the Commune were divided into a majority, the Blanquists, who had also been predominant in the Central Committee of the National Guard; and a minority, members of the International Working Men's Association, chiefly consisting of adherents of the Proudhon school of socialism. The great majority of the Blanquists at that time were socialists only by revolutionary and proletarian instinct; only a few had attained greater clarity on the essential principles, through Vaillant, who was familiar with German scientific socialism. It is therefore comprehensible that in the economic sphere much was left undone which, according to our view today, the Commune ought to have done. The hardest thing to understand is certainly the holy awe with which they remained standing respectfully outside the gates of the Bank of France. This was also a serious political mistake. The bank in the hands of the Commune—this would have been worth more than ten thousand hostages. It would have meant the pressure of the whole of the French bourgeoisie on the Versailles government in favour of peace with the Commune. But what is still more wonderful is the correctness of so much that was actually done by the Commune, composed as it was of Blanquists and Proudhonists. Naturally, the Proudhonists were chiefly responsible for the economic decrees of the Commune, both for their praiseworthy and their unpraiseworthy aspects; as the Blanquists were for its political actions and omissions. And in both cases the irony of history willed—as is usual when doctrinaires come to the helm—that both did the opposite of what the doctrines of their school prescribed.

Proudhon, the Socialist of the small peasant and master-craftsman, regarded association with positive hatred. He said of it that there was more bad than good in it; that it was by nature sterile, even harmful, because it was a fetter on the freedom of the workers; that it was a pure dogma, unproductive and burdensome, in conflict as much with the freedom of the workers as with economy of labour; that its disadvantages multiplied more swiftly than its advantages; that, as compared with it, competition, division of labour and private property were economic forces. Only for the exceptional cases—as Proudhon called them—of large-scale industry and large industrial units, such as railways, was there any place for the association of workers. (*Cf. Idée Générale de la Révolution, 3 étude.*)

By 1871, even in Paris, the centre of handicrafts, large-scale industry had already so much ceased to be an exceptional case that by far the most important decree of the Commune instituted an organisation of large-scale industry and even of manufacture which was not based only on the association of workers in each factory, but also aimed at combining all these associations in one great union; in short an organisation which, as Marx quite rightly says in *The Civil War,* must necessarily have led in the end to communism, that is to say, the direct antithesis of the Proudhon doctrine. And, therefore, the Commune was also the grave of the Proudhon school of socialism. Today this school has vanished from French working class circles; among them now, among the Possibilists [11] no less than among the "Marxists," Marx's theory rules unchallenged. Only among the "radical" bourgeoisie are there still Proudhonists.

The Blanquists fared no better. Brought up in the school of conspiracy, and held together by the strict discipline which went with it, they started out from the viewpoint that a relatively small number of resolute, well-organised men would be able, at a given favourable moment, not only to seize the helm of state, but also by energetic and relentless action, to keep power until they succeeded in drawing the mass of the people into the revolution and ranging them round the small band of leaders. This conception involved, above all, the strictest dictatorship, and centralisation of all power in the hands of the new revolutionary government. And what did the Commune, with its majority of these same Blanquists, actually do? In all its proclamations to the French in the provinces, it proposed to them a free federation of all French Communes with Paris, a national organisation, which for the first time was really to be created by the nation itself. It was precisely the oppressing power of the former centralised government, army, political police and bureaucracy, which Napoleon had created in 1798 and since then had been taken over by every new government as a welcome instrument and used against its opponents, it was precisely this power which was to fall everywhere, just as it had already fallen in Paris.

From the outset the Commune was compelled to recognise that the working class, once come to power, could not manage with the old state machine; that in order not to lose again its only just conquered supremacy, this working class must, on the one hand, do away with all the old repressive machinery previously used against it itself, and, on the other, safeguard itself against its own deputies and officials, by declaring them all, without exception, subject to recall at any moment. What had been the characteristic attribute of the former state? Society had created its own organs to look after its common interests, originally through simple division of labour. But these organs, at whose head was the state power, had in the course of time, in pursuance of their own special interests, transformed themselves from the servants of society into the masters of society, as can be seen, for example, not only in the hereditary monarchy, but equally also in the democratic republic. Nowhere do "politicians" form a more separate, powerful section of the nation than in North America. There, each of the two great parties[12] which alternately succeed each other in power is itself in turn controlled by people who make a business of politics, who speculate on seats in the legislative assemblies of the Union as well as of the separate states, or who make a living by carrying on agitation for their party and on its victory are rewarded with positions.

It is well known that the Americans have been striving for thirty years to shake off this yoke, which has become intolerable, and that in spite of all they can do they continue to sink ever deeper in this swamp of corruption. It is precisely in America that we see best how there takes place this process of the state power making itself independent in relation to society, whose mere instrument it was originally intended to be. Here there exists no dynasty, no nobility, no standing army, beyond the few men keeping watch on the Indians, no bureaucracy with permanent posts or the right to pensions. And nevertheless we find here two great gangs of political speculators, who alternately take possession of the state power and exploit it by the most corrupt means and for the most corrupt ends —and the nation is powerless against these two great cartels of politicians, who are ostensibly its servants, but in reality exploit and plunder it.

Against this transformation of the state and the organs of the state from servants of society into masters of society—an inevitable transformation in all previous states—the Commune made use of two infallible expedients. In the first place, it filled all posts— administrative, judicial and educational—by election on the basis of universal suffrage of all concerned, with the right of the same electors to recall their delegate at any time. And in the second place, all officials, high or low, were paid only the wages received by other workers. The highest salary paid by the Commune to anyone was 6,000 francs. In this way an effective barrier to place-hunting and careerism was set up, even apart from the binding mandates to delegates to representative bodies which were also added in profusion.

This shattering of the former state power and its replacement by a new and really democratic state is described in detail in the third section of *The Civil War*. But it was necessary to dwell briefly here once more on some of its features, because in Germany particularly the superstitious belief in the state has been carried over from philosophy into the general consciousness of the bourgeoisie and even to many workers. According to the philosophical notion, the state is the "realisation of the idea" or the Kingdom of God on earth, translated into philosophical terms, the sphere in which eternal truth and justice is or should be realised. And from this follows a superstitious reverence for the state and everything connected with it, which takes root the more readily as people from their childhood are accustomed to imagine that the affairs and interests common to the whole of society could not be looked after otherwise than as they have been looked after in the past, that is, through the state and its well-paid officials. And people think they have taken quite an extraordinarily bold step forward when they have rid themselves of belief in hereditary monarchy and swear by the democratic republic. In reality, however, the state is nothing but a machine for the oppression of one class by another, and indeed in the democratic republic no less than in the monarchy; and at best an evil inherited by the proletariat after its victorious struggle for class supremacy, whose worst sides the proletariat, just like the Commune, cannot avoid having to lop off at the earliest possible moment, until such time as a new generation, reared in new and free social conditions, will be able to throw the entire lumber of the state on the scrap-heap.

Of late, the Social-Democratic philistine [18] has once more been filled with wholesome terror at the words: Dictatorship of the Proletariat. Well and good, gentlemen, do you want to know what this dictatorship looks like? Look at the Paris Commune. That was the Dictatorship of the Proletariat.

FREDERICK ENGELS

London, on the twentieth anniversary
of the Paris Commune, March 18, 1891.

I

FIRST ADDRESS OF THE GENERAL COUNCIL ON THE
FRANCO-PRUSSIAN WAR

*To the Members of the International Working Men's Association
in Europe and the United States*

IN THE Inaugural Address of the International Working Men's
Association, of November 1864, we said: "If the emancipation of
the working classes requires their fraternal concurrence, how are
they to fulfil that great mission with a foreign policy in pursuit of
criminal designs, playing upon national prejudices, and squan-
dering in piratical wars the people's blood and treasure?" We
defined the foreign policy aimed at by the International in these
words: "Vindicate the simple laws of morals and justice, which
ought to govern the relations of private individuals, as the laws
paramount of the intercourse of nations."

No wonder that Louis Bonaparte, who usurped his power by
exploiting the war of classes in France, and perpetuated it by
periodical wars abroad, should, from the first, have treated the
International as a dangerous foe. On the eve of the plebiscite [14] he
ordered a raid on the members of the Administrative Committees of
the International Working Men's Association throughout France,
at Paris, Lyons, Rouen, Marseilles, Brest, etc.,[15] on the pretext that
the International was a secret society dabbling in a *complot* for
his assassination, a pretext soon after exposed in its full absurdity
by his own judges. What was the real crime of the French branches
of the International? They told the French people publicly and
emphatically that voting the plebiscite was voting despotism at
home and war abroad. It has been, in fact, their work that in all
the great towns, in all the industrial centres of France, the working
class rose like one man to reject the plebiscite. Unfortunately the

23

balance was turned by the heavy ignorance of the rural districts. The stock exchanges, the cabinets, the ruling classes and the press of Europe celebrated the plebiscite as a signal victory of the French emperor over the French working class; and it was the signal for the assassination, not of an individual, but of nations.

The war plot of July 1870 [16] is but an amended edition of the *coup d'état* of December 1851. At first view the thing seemed so absurd that France would not believe in its real good earnest. It rather believed the deputy denouncing the ministerial war talk as a mere stock-jobbing trick. When, on July 15, war was at last officially announced to the *Corps Législatif,* the whole Opposition refused to vote the preliminary subsidies—even Thiers branded it as "detestable"; all the independent journals of Paris condemned it, and, wonderful to relate, the provincial press joined in almost unanimously.

Meanwhile, the Paris members of the International had again set to work. In the *Reveil* of July 12 they published their manifesto "to the Workmen of all Nations," from which we extract the following few passages:

"Once more," they say, "on the pretext of European equilibrium, of national honour, the peace of the world is menaced by political ambitions. French, German, Spanish workmen! Let our voices unite in one cry of reprobation against war! ... War for a question of preponderance or a dynasty can, in the eyes of workmen, be nothing but a criminal absurdity. In answer to the warlike proclamations of those who exempt themselves from the blood tax, and find in public misfortunes a source of fresh speculations, we protest, we who want peace, labour and liberty! ... Brothers in Germany! Our division would only result in the complete triumph of the despotism on both sides of the Rhine.... Workmen of all countries! Whatever may for the present become of our common efforts, we, the members of the International Working Men's Association, who know of no frontiers, we send you, as a pledge of indissoluble solidarity, the good wishes and the salutations of the workmen of France."

This manifesto of our Paris section was followed by numerous similar French addresses, of which we can here only quote the declaration of Neuilly-sur-Seine, published in the *Marseillaise* of July 22:

"The war, is it just? No! The war, is it national? No! It is merely dynastic. In the name of humanity, or democracy, and the true interests of France, we adhere completely and energetically to the protestation of the International against the war."

These protestations expressed the true sentiments of the French working people, as was soon shown by a curious incident. *The Band of the Tenth of December,*[17] first organised under the presidency of Louis Bonaparte, having been masqueraded into *blouses* and let loose on the streets of Paris, there to perform the contortions of war fever, the real workmen of the Faubourgs came forward with public peace demonstrations so overwhelming that Pietri, the Prefect of Police, thought it prudent to stop at once all further street politics, on the plea that the real Paris people had given sufficient vent to their pent-up patriotism and exuberant war enthusiasm.

Whatever may be the incidents of Louis Bonaparte's war with Prussia, the death-knell of the Second Empire has already sounded at Paris. It will end, as it began, by a parody. But let us not forget that it is the governments and the ruling classes of Europe who enabled Louis Bonaparte to play during eighteen years the ferocious farce of the *Restored Empire.*

On the German side, the war is a war of defence;[18] but who put Germany to the necessity of defending herself? Who enabled Louis Bonaparte to wage war upon her? Prussia! It was Bismarck who conspired with that very same Louis Bonaparte for the purpose of crushing popular opposition at home, and annexing Germany to the Hohenzollern dynasty. If the battle of Sadowa[19] had been lost instead of being won, French battalions would have overrun Germany as the allies of Prussia. After her victory, did Prussia dream one moment of opposing a free Germany to an enslaved France? Just the contrary. While carefully preserving all the native beauties of her old system, she super-added all the tricks of the Second Empire, its real despotism and its mock democratism, its political shams and its financial jobs, its high-flown talk and its low *legerdemains*. The Bonapartist regime, which till then only flourished on one side of the Rhine, had now got its counterfeit on the other. From such a state of things, what else could result but *war?*

If the German working class allows the present war to lose its strictly defensive character and to degenerate into a war against the French people, victory or defeat will prove alike disastrous. All the miseries that befell Germany after her war of independence will revive with accumulated intensity.

The principles of the International are, however, too widely spread and too firmly rooted amongst the German working class to apprehend such a sad consummation. The voices of the French workmen had re-echoed from Germany. A mass meeting of workmen, held at Brunswick on July 16, expressed its full concurrence with the Paris manifesto, spurned the idea of national antagonism to France, and wound up its resolutions with these words:

"We are enemies of all wars, but above all of dynastic wars.[20] ... With deep sorrow and grief we are forced to undergo a defensive war as an unavoidable evil; but we call, at the same time, upon the whole German working class to render the recurrence of such an immense social misfortune impossible by vindicating for the peoples themselves the power to decide on peace and war, and making them masters of their own destinies."

At Chemnitz, a meeting of delegates, representing 50,000 Saxon workmen, adopted unanimously a resolution to this effect:

"In the name of the German Democracy, and especially of the workmen forming the Democratic Socialist Party, we declare the present war to be exclusively dynastic. . . . We are happy to grasp the fraternal hand stretched out to us by the workmen of France. . . . Mindful of the watchword of the International Working Men's Association: *Proletarians of all countries, unite,* we shall never forget that the workmen of *all* countries are our *friends* and the despots of *all* countries our *enemies.*"

The Berlin branch of the International has also replied to the Paris manifesto:

"We," they say, "join with heart and hand your protestation.... Solemnly we promise that neither the sound of the trumpet, nor the roar of the cannon, neither victory nor defeat, shall divert us from our common work for the union of the children of toil of all countries."

Be it so!

In the background of this suicidal strike looms the dark figure of Russia. It is an ominous sign that the signal for the present war should have been given at the moment when the Moscovite government had just finished its strategic lines of railway and was already massing troops in the direction of the Pruth. Whatever sympathy the Germans may justly claim in a war of defence against Bonapartist aggression, they would forfeit at once by allowing the Prussian government to call for, or accept the help of, the Cossack. Let them remember that after their war of independence against the first Napoleon, Germany lay for generations prostrate at the feet of the tsar.[21]

The English working class stretch the hand of fellowship to the French and German working people. They feel deeply convinced that whatever turn the impending horrid war may take, the alliance of the working classes of all countries will ultimately kill war. The very fact that while official France and Germany are rushing into a fratricidal feud, the workmen of France and Germany send each other messages of peace and goodwill; this great fact, unparalleled in the history of the past, opens the vista of a brighter future. It proves that in contrast to old society, with its economical miseries and its political delirium, a new society is springing up, whose International rule will be *Peace,* because its national ruler will be everywhere the same—*Labour!* The pioneer of that new society is the International Working Men's Association.

July 23, 1870.

II

In our first manifesto of the 23rd of July we said:

"The death-knell of the Second Empire has already sounded at Paris.
It will end, as it began, by a parody. But let us not forget that it is the
governments and the ruling classes of Europe who enabled Louis
Napoleon to play during eighteen years the ferocious farce of the
Restored Empire."

Thus, even before war operations had actually set in, we treated
the Bonapartist bubble as a thing of the past.

If we were not mistaken as to the vitality of the Second Empire,
we were not wrong in our apprehension lest the German war
should "lose its strictly defensive character and degenerate into
a war against the French people." The war of defence ended, in
point of fact, with the surrender of Louis Bonaparte, the Sedan
capitulation, and the proclamation of the republic at Paris.[22] But
long before these events, the very moment that the utter rottenness
of the imperialist arms became evident, the Prussian military
camarilla had resolved upon conquest. There lay an ugly obstacle
in their way—*King William's own proclamations at the commencement of the war.* In his speech from the throne to the North German Diet, he had solemnly declared to make war upon the emperor
of the French and not upon the French people. On August 11 he
had issued a manifesto to the French nation, where he said: "The
Emperor Napoleon having made by land and sea an attack on the
German nation, which desired and still desires to live in peace with
the French people, I have assumed the command of the German
armies *to repel his aggression,* and I have been led by *military events
to cross the frontiers of France.*" Not content to assert the defensive
character of the war by the statement that he only assumed the
command of the German armies *"to repel aggression,"* he added
that he was only "led by military events" to cross the frontiers of

France. A defensive war does, of course, not exclude offensive operations, dictated by military events.

Thus, the pious king stood pledged before France and the world to a strictly defensive war. How to release him from his solemn pledge? The stage managers had to exhibit him as reluctantly yielding to the irresistible behest of the German nation. They at once gave the cue to the liberal German middle class, with its professors, its capitalists, its aldermen and its penmen. That middle class, which, in its struggles for civil liberty, had, from 1846 to 1870, been exhibiting an unexampled spectacle of irresolution, incapacity and cowardice, felt, of course, highly delighted to bestride the European scene as the roaring lion of German patriotism. It re-vindicated its civic independence by affecting to force upon the Prussian government the secret designs of that same government. It does penance for its long-continued and almost religious faith in Louis Bonaparte's infallibility, by shouting for the dismemberment of the French republic. Let us for a moment listen to the special pleadings of those stout-hearted patriots!

They dare not pretend that the people of Alsace and Lorraine pant for the German embrace; quite the contrary. To punish their French patriotism, Strasbourg, a town with an independent citadel commanding it, has for six days been wantonly and fiendishly bombarded by "German" explosive shells, setting it on fire, and killing great numbers of its defenceless inhabitants! Yet, the soil of those provinces once upon a time belonged to the whilom German empire. Hence, it seems, the soil and the human beings grown on it must be confiscated as imprescriptible German property. If the map of Europe is to be re-made in the antiquary's vein, let us by no means forget that the Elector of Brandenburg, for his Prussian dominions, was the vassal of the Polish republic.

The more knowing patriots, however, require Alsace and the German-speaking part of Lorraine as a "material guarantee" against French aggression. As this contemptible plea has bewildered many weak-minded people, we are bound to enter more fully upon it.

There is no doubt that the general configuration of Alsace, as compared with the opposite bank of the Rhine, and the presence

of a large fortified town like Strasbourg, about halfway between
Basle and Germersheim, very much favour a French invasion of
South Germany, while they offer peculiar difficulties to an invasion
of France from South Germany. There is, further, no doubt that
the addition of Alsace and German-speaking Lorraine would give
South Germany a much stronger frontier, inasmuch as she would
then be master of the crest of the Vosges mountains in its whole
length, and of the fortresses which cover its northern passes. If
Metz were annexed as well, France would certainly for the moment
be deprived of her two principal bases of operation against Germany, but that would not prevent her from constructing a fresh
one at Nancy or Verdun. While Germany owns Coblenz, Mayence,
Germersheim, Rastatt, and Ulm, all bases of operation against
France, and plentifully made use of in this war, with what show
of fair play can she begrudge France Strasbourg and Metz, the
only two fortresses of any importance she has on that side? Moreover, Strasbourg endangers South Germany only, while South
Germany is a separate power from North Germany. From 1792 to
1795 South Germany was never invaded from that direction, because
Prussia was a party to the war against the French Revolution; but
as soon as Prussia made a peace of her own in 1795, and left the
South to shift for itself, the invasions of South Germany with
Strasbourg for a base began and continued till 1809. The fact is, a
united Germany can always render Strasbourg and any French
army in Alsace innocuous by concentrating all her troops, as was
done in the present war, between Saarlouis and Landau, and advancing, or accepting battle, on the line of road between Mayence
and Metz. While the mass of the German troops is stationed there,
any French army advancing from Strasbourg into South Germany
would be outflanked, and have its communications threatened. If
the present campaign has proved anything, it is the facility of
invading France from Germany.

But, in good faith, is it not altogether an absurdity and an
anachronism to make military considerations the principle by which
the boundaries of nations are to be fixed? If this rule were to
prevail, Austria would still be entitled to Venetia and the line

of the Mincio, and France to the line of the Rhine, in order to
protect Paris, which lies certainly more open to an attack from
the northeast than Berlin does from the southwest. If limits are to
be fixed by military interests, there will be no end to claims, be-
'cause every military line is necessarily faulty, and may be improved
by annexing some more outlying territory; and, moreover, they can
never be fixed finally and fairly, because they always must be
imposed by the conqueror upon the conquered, and consequently
carry within them the seed of fresh wars.

Such is the lesson of all history. Thus with nations as with
individuals. To deprive them of the power of offence, you must
deprive them of the means of defence. You must not only garrote,
but murder. If every conqueror took "material guarantees" for
breaking the sinews of a nation, the first Napoleon did so by the
Tilsit Treaty,[23] and the way he executed it against Prussia and
the rest of Germany. Yet, a few years later, his gigantic power split
like a rotten reed upon the German people. What are the "material
guarantees" Prussia, in her wildest dreams, can or dare impose
upon France, compared to the "material guarantees" the first Napoleon had wrenched from herself? The result will not prove
the less disastrous. History will measure its retribution, not by the
extent of the square miles conquered from France, but by the
intensity of the crime of reviving, in the second half of the nine-
teenth century, *the policy of conquest!*

But, say the mouthpieces of Teutonic patriotism, you must not
confound Germans with Frenchmen. What *we* want is not glory,
but safety. The Germans are an essentially peaceful people. In
their sober guardianship, conquest itself changes from a condition
of future war into a pledge of perpetual peace. Of course, it is not
Germans that invaded France in 1792, for the sublime purpose of
bayonetting the revolution of the eighteenth century. It is not
Germans that befouled their hands by the subjugation of Italy, the
oppression of Hungary, and the dismemberment of Poland. Their
present military system, which divides the whole able-bodied male
population into two parts—one standing army on service, and another standing army on furlough, both equally bound in passive

obedience to rulers by divine right—such a military system is, of course, "a material guarantee," for keeping the peace and the ultimate goal of civilising tendencies! In Germany, as everywhere else, the sycophants of the powers that be poison the popular mind by the incense of mendacious self praise.

Indignant as they pretend to be at the sight of French fortresses in Metz and Strasbourg, those German patriots see no harm in the vast system of Moscovite fortifications at Warsaw, Modlin, and Ivangorod. While gloating at the terrors of imperialist invasion, they blink at the infamy of autocratic tutelage.

As in 1865 promises were exchanged between Louis Bonaparte and Bismarck, so in 1870 promises have been exchanged between Gorchakov [24] and Bismarck. As Louis Bonaparte flattered himself that the War of 1866, resulting in the common exhaustion of Austria and Prussia, would make him the supreme arbiter of Germany, so Alexander flattered himself that the War of 1870, resulting in the common exhaustion of Germany and France, would make him the supreme arbiter of the Western continent. As the Second Empire thought the North German Confederation incompatible with its existence, so autocratic Russia must think herself endangered by a German empire under Prussian leadership. Such is the law of the old political system. Within its pale the gain of one state is the loss of the other. The tsar's paramount influence over Europe roots in his traditional hold on Germany. At a moment when in Russia herself volcanic social agencies threaten to shake the very base of autocracy, could the tsar afford to bear with such a loss of foreign prestige? Already the Moscovite journals repeat the language of the Bonapartist journals after the War of 1866.[25] Do the Teuton patriots really believe that liberty and peace will be guaranteed to Germany by forcing France into the arms of Russia? If the fortune of her arms, the arrogance of success, and dynastic intrigue lead Germany to a spoliation of French territory, there will then only remain two courses open to her. She must at all risks become the *avowed* tool of Russian aggrandisement, or, after some short respite, make again ready for another "defensive" war, not one of those new-fangled "localised" wars, but a *war of races*—a war with the combined Slavonian and Roman races.

The German working class have resolutely supported the war, which it was not in their power to prevent, as a war for German independence and the liberation of France and Europe from that pestilential incubus, the Second Empire. It was the German workmen who, together with the rural labourers, furnished the sinews and muscles of heroic hosts, leaving behind their half-starved families. Decimated by the battles abroad, they will be once more decimated by misery at home. In their turn they are now coming forward to ask for "guarantees"—guarantees that their immense sacrifices have not been bought in vain, that they have conquered liberty, that the victory over the imperialist armies will not, as in 1815, be turned into the defeat of the German people; and, as the first of these guarantees, they claim an *honourable peace for France,* and the *recognition of the French republic.*

The Central Committee of the German Socialist-Democratic Workmen's Party issued on September 5 a manifesto,[26] energetically insisting upon these guarantees.

"We," they say, "protest against the annexation of Alsace and Lorraine. And we are conscious of speaking in the name of the German working class. In the common interest of France and Germany, in the interest of western civilisation against eastern barbarism the German workmen will not patiently tolerate the annexation of Alsace and Lorraine.... We shall faithfully stand by our fellow workmen in all countries for the common international cause of the proletariat!"

Unfortunately, we cannot feel sanguine of their immediate success. If the French workmen amidst peace failed to stop the aggressor, are the German workmen more likely to stop the victor amidst the clamour of arms? The German workmen's manifesto demands the extradition of Louis Bonaparte as a common felon to the French republic. Their rulers are, on the contrary, already trying hard to restore him to the Tuileries as the best man to ruin France. However that may be, history will prove that the German working class are not made of the same malleable stuff as the German middle class. They will do their duty.

Like them, we hail the advent of the republic in France, but at the same time we labour under misgivings which we hope will prove groundless. That republic has not subverted the throne, but only taken its place become vacant. It has been proclaimed, not as a social conquest, but as a national measure of defence. It is in the hands of a Provisional Government composed partly of notorious Orleanists, partly of middle class republicans, upon some of whom the insurrection of June 1848 has left its indelible stigma. The division of labour amongst the members of that government looks awkward. The Orleanists have seized the strongholds of the army and the police, while to the professed republicans have fallen the talking departments. Some of their first acts go far to show that they have inherited from the empire, not only ruins, but also its dread of the working class. If eventual impossibilities are in wild phraseology promised in the name of the republic, is it not with a view to prepare the cry for a "possible" government! Is the republic, by some of its middle class undertakers, not intended to serve as a mere stop-gap and bridge over an Orleanist restoration?

The French working class moves, therefore, under circumstances of extreme difficulty. Any attempt at upsetting the new government in the present crisis, when the enemy is almost knocking at the doors of Paris, would be a desperate folly.[27] The French workmen must perform their duties as citizens; but, at the same time, they must not allow themselves to be swayed by the national *souvenirs* of 1792,[28] as the French peasants allowed themselves to be deluded by the national *souvenirs* of the First Empire.[29] They have not to recapitulate the past, but to build up the future. Let them calmly and resolutely improve the opportunities of republican liberty, for the work of their own class organisation. It will gift them with fresh herculean powers for the regeneration of France, and our common task—the emancipation of labour. Upon their energies and wisdom hinges the fate of the republic.

The English workmen have already taken measures to overcome, by a wholesome pressure from without, the reluctance of their government to recognise the French republic.[30] The present dilatoriness of the British government is probably intended to atone for the Anti-Jacobin war [1792] [31] and the former indecent haste in sanctioning the *coup d'état*. The English workmen call also upon their government to oppose by all its power the dismemberment of France, which a part of the English press is shameless enough to howl for. It is the same press that for twenty years deified Louis Bonaparte as the providence of Europe, that frantically cheered on the slaveholders to rebellion.[32] Now, as then, it drudges for the slaveholder.

Let the sections of the *International Working Men's Association* in every country stir the working classes to action. If they forsake their duty, if they remain passive, the present tremendous war will be but the harbinger of still deadlier international feuds, and lead in every nation to a renewed triumph over the workman by the lords of the sword, of the soil and of capital.

Vive la République!

THE GENERAL COUNCIL

ROBERT APPLEGARTH, MARTIN J. BOON, FRED. BRADNICK, CAIHIL, JOHN HALES, WILLIAM HALES, GEORGE HARRIS, FRED. LESSNER, LAYSATINE, B. LUCRAFT, GEORGE MILNER, THOMAS MOTTERSHEAD, CHARLES MURRAY, GEORGE ODGER, JAMES PARNELL, PFANDER, RUHL, JOSEPH SHEPHERD, COWELL STEPNEY, STOLL, SCHMITZ.

CORRESPONDING SECRETARIES:

EUGENE DUPONT, *for France*

HERMANN JUNG, *for Switzerland Holland and Spain*

A. SERRAILLER, *for Belgium*

KARL MARX, *for Germany and Russia*

GIOVANNI BORA, *for Italy*

ZEVY MAURICE, *for Hungary*

ANTON ZABICKI, *for Poland*

JAMES COHEN, *for Denmark*

J. G. ECCARIUS, *for the United States*

WILLIAM TOWNSEND, *Chairman*

JOHN WESTON, *Treasurer*

J. GEORGE ECCARIUS, *General Secretary*

Office: 256 HIGH HOLBORN, LONDON, W.C., *September 9, 1870*

ADDRESS OF THE GENERAL COUNCIL OF THE INTERNATIONAL WORKING MEN'S ASSOCIATION ON *THE CIVIL WAR IN FRANCE, 1871*

To All the Members of the Association in Europe and the United States

I

ON THE 4th of September, 1870, when the working men of Paris proclaimed the republic, which was almost instantaneously acclaimed throughout France, without a single voice of dissent, a cabal of place-hunting barristers, with Thiers for their statesman and Trochu for their general, took hold of the Hôtel de Ville. At that time they were imbued with so fanatical a faith in the mission of Paris to represent France in all epochs of historical crisis, that, to legitimate their usurped titles as governors of France, they thought it quite sufficient to produce their lapsed mandates as representatives of Paris. In our second address on the late war, five days after the rise of these men, we told you who they were. Yet, in the turmoil of surprise, with the real leaders of the working class still shut up in Bonapartist prisons and the Prussians already marching upon Paris, Paris bore with their assumption of power, on the express condition that it was to be wielded for the single purpose of national defence. Paris, however, was not to be defended without arming its working class, organising them into an effective force, and training their ranks by the war itself. But Paris armed was the revolution armed. A victory of Paris over the Prussian aggressor would have been a victory of the French workmen over the French capitalist and his state parasites. In this conflict between national duty and class interest, the Government of National

36

Defence did not hesitate one moment to turn into a Government of National Defection.

The first step they took was to send Thiers on a roving tour to all the courts of Europe, there to beg mediation by offering the barter of the republic for a king. Four months after the commencement of the siege, when they thought the opportune moment come for breaking the first word of capitulation, Trochu, in the presence of Jules Favre and others of his colleagues, addressed the assembled mayors of Paris in these terms:

"The first question put to me by my colleagues on the very evening of the 4th of September was this: Paris, can it, with any chance of success, stand a siege by the Prussian army? I did not hesitate to answer in the negative. Some of my colleagues here present will warrant the truth of my words and the persistence of my opinion. I told them, in these very terms, that, under the existing state of things, the attempt of Paris to hold out a siege by the Prussian army would be a folly. Without doubt, I added, it would be an heroic folly; but that would be all.... The events [managed by himself] have not given the lie to my prevision."

This nice little speech of Trochu was afterwards published by M. Carbon, one of the mayors present.

Thus, on the very evening of the proclamation of the republic, Trochu's "plan" was known to his colleagues to be the capitulation of Paris. If national defence had been more than a pretext for the personal government of Thiers, Favre and Co., the upstarts of the 4th of September would have abdicated on the 5th—would have initiated the Paris people into Trochu's "plan," and called upon them to surrender at once, or to take their own fate into their own hands. Instead of this, the infamous impostors resolved upon curing the heroic folly of Paris by a regimen of famine and broken heads, and to dupe her in the meanwhile by ranting manifestoes, holding forth that Trochu, "the governor of Paris, will never capitulate," and Jules Favre, the foreign minister, will "not cede an inch of our territory, nor a stone of our fortresses."

In a letter to Gambetta, that very same Jules Favre avows that what they were "defending" against were not the Prussian soldiers, but the working men of Paris. During the whole continuance of the siege the Bonapartist cut-throats, whom Trochu had wisely intrusted with the command of the Paris army, exchanged, in their intimate correspondence, ribald jokes at the well-understood mockery of defence. (See, for instance, the correspondence of Alphonse Simon Guiod, supreme commander of the artillery of the Army of Defence of Paris and Grand Cross of the Legion of Honour, to Suzanne, general of division of artillery, a correspondence published by the *Journal officiel* of the Commune.) The mask of imposture was at last dropped on the 28th of January, 1871. With the true heroism of utter self-debasement, the Government of National Defence, in their capitulation, came out as the government of France by Bismarck's prisoners—a part so base that Louis Bonaparte himself had, at Sedan, shrunk from accepting it. After the events of the 18th of March on their wild flight to Versailles, the *capitulards* left in the hands of Paris the documentary evidence of their treason, to destroy which, as the Commune says in its manifesto to the provinces, "those men would not recoil from battering Paris into a heap of ruins washed by a sea of blood."

To be eagerly bent upon such a consummation, some of the leading members of the Government of Defence had, besides, most peculiar reasons of their own.

Shortly after the conclusion of the armistice, M. Millière, one of the representatives of Paris to the National Assembly, now shot by express order of Jules Favre, published a series of authentic legal documents in proof that Jules Favre, living in concubinage with the wife of a drunken resident at Algiers, had, by a most daring concoction of forgeries, spread over many years, contrived to grasp, in the name of the children of his adultery, a large succession, which made him a rich man, and that, in a lawsuit undertaken by the legitimate heirs, he only escaped exposure by the connivance of the Bonapartist tribunals. As these dry legal documents were not to be got rid of by any amount of rhetorical horse-power, Jules Favre, for the first time in his life, held his tongue, quietly awaiting the outbreak of the civil war, in order, then, frantically to denounce the people of Paris as a band of escaped convicts in utter revolt against family, religion, order and property. This same forger had hardly got into power, after the 4th of September, when he sympathetically let loose upon society Pic and Taillefer, convicted, even under the empire, of forgery in the scandalous affair of the "Etendard." One of these men, Taillefer, having dared to return to Paris under the Commune, was at once reinstated in prison; and then Jules Favre exclaimed, from the tribune of the National Assembly, that Paris was setting free all her jailbirds!

Ernest Picard, the Joe Miller of the Government of National Defence, who appointed himself finance minister of the republic after having in vain striven to become the home minister of the empire, is the brother of one Arthur Picard, an individual expelled from the Paris *Bourse* as a blackleg (see report of the Prefecture of Police, dated 13th July, 1867), and convicted, on his own confession, of a theft of 300,000 francs, while manager of one of the branches of the *Société Générale,* Rue Palestro, No. 5 (see report of the Prefecture of Police, 11th December, 1868). This Arthur Picard was made by Ernest Picard the editor of his paper, *l'Electeur Libre*. While the common run of stockjobbers were led astray by the official lies of this finance office paper, Arthur was running backwards and forwards between the finance office and the *Bourse,* there to discount the disasters of the French army. The whole financial correspondence of that worthy pair of brothers fell into the hands of the Commune.

Jules Ferry, a penniless barrister before the 4th of September, contrived, as mayor of Paris during the siege, to job a fortune out of famine. The day on which he would have to give an account of his maladministration would be the day of his conviction.

These men, then, could find in the ruins of Paris only their tickets-of-leave: they were the very men Bismarck wanted. With the help of some shuffling of cards, Thiers, hitherto the secret prompter of the government, now appeared at its head, with the ticket-of-leave men for his ministers.

Thiers, that monstrous gnome, has charmed the French bourgeoisie for almost half a century, because he is the most consummate intellectual expression of their own class corruption. Before he became a statesman he had already proved his lying powers as an historian. The chronicle of his public life is the record of the misfortunes of France. Banded, before 1830, with the republicans, he slipped into office under Louis Philippe by betraying his protector Lafitte, ingratiating himself with the king by exciting mob riots against the clergy, during which the church of Saint Germain l'Auxerrois and the Archbishop's palace were plundered, and by acting the minister-spy upon, and the jail-*accoucheur* of the Duchess de Berri. The massacre of the republicans in the Rue Transnonain,[33] and the subsequent infamous laws of September against the press and the right of association, were his work. Reappearing as the chief of the cabinet in March 1840, he astonished France with his plan of fortifying France. To the republicans, who denounced this plan as a sinister plot against the liberty of Paris, he replied from the tribune of the Chamber of Deputies:

"What! to fancy that any works of fortification could ever endanger liberty! And first of all you calumniate any possible government in supposing that it could some day attempt to maintain itself by bombarding the capital; ... but that government would be a hundred times more impossible after its victory than before."

Indeed, no government would ever have dared to bombard Paris from the forts but that government which had previously surrendered these forts to the Prussians.

When King Bomba[34] tried his hand at Palermo, in January 1848, Thiers, then long since out of office, again rose in the Chamber of Deputies:

"You know, gentlemen, what is happening at Palermo. You, all of you, shake with horror [in the parliamentary sense] on hearing that during forty-eight hours a large town has been bombarded—by whom? Was it by a foreign enemy exercising the rights of war? No, gentlemen, it was by its own government. And why? Because the unfortunate town demanded its right. Well, then, for the demand of its rights it has got forty-eight hours of bombardment. . . . Allow me to appeal to the opinion of Europe. It is doing a service to mankind to arise, and to make reverberate, from what is perhaps the greatest tribune in Europe, some words [indeed words] of indignation against such acts. . . . When the Regent Espartero, who had rendered services to his country [which M. Thiers never did] intended bombarding Barcelona, in order to suppress its insurrection, there arose from all parts of the world a general outcry of indignation."

Eighteen months afterwards, M. Thiers was amongst the fiercest defenders of the bombardment of Rome by a French army. In fact, the fault of King Bomba seems to have consisted in this only, that he limited his bombardment to forty-eight hours.

A few days before the Revolution of February, fretting at the long exile from place and pelf to which Guizot had condemned him, and sniffing in the air the scent of an approaching popular commotion, Thiers, in that pseudo-heroic style which won him the nickname of *Mirabeau-mouche,* declared, to the Chamber of Deputies:

"I am of the party of revolution, not only in France, but in Europe. I wish the government of the revolution to remain in the hands of moderate men ... but if that government should fall into the hands of ardent minds, even into those of radicals, I shall, for all that, not desert my cause. I shall always be of the party of the revolution."

The Revolution of February came. Instead of displacing the Guizot Cabinet by the Thiers Cabinet, as the little man had dreamt, it superseded Louis Philippe by the republic. On the first day of the popular victory he carefully hid himself, forgetting that the contempt of the working men screened him from their hatred. Still, with his legendary courage, he continued to shy the public stage, until the June massacres [35] had cleared it for his sort of action. Then he became the leading mind of the "Party of Order" and its parliamentary republic, that anonymous interregnum, in which all the rival factions of the ruling class conspired together to crush the people, and conspired against each other to restore to each of them its own monarchy. Then, as now, Thiers denounced the republicans as the only obstacle to the consolidation of the republic; then, as now, he spoke to the republic as the hangman spoke to Don Carlos: [36] "I shall assassinate thee, but for thy own good." Now, as then, he will have to exclaim on the day after his victory: *L'Empire est fait*—the empire is consummated. Despite his hypocritical homilies about necessary liberties and his personal grudge against Louis Bonaparte, who had made a dupe of him, and kicked out parliamentarism—and outside of its factitious atmosphere the little man is conscious of withering into nothingness—he had a hand in all the infamies of the Second Empire, from the occupation of Rome by French troops to the war with Prussia, which he incited by his fierce invective against German unity—not as a cloak of Prussian despotism, but as an encroachment upon the vested right of France in German disunion. Fond of brandishing with his dwarfish arms in the face of Europe the sword of the first Napoleon, whose historical shoeblack he had become,[37] his foreign policy always culminated in the utter humiliation of France, from the London convention of 1840 to the Paris capitulation of 1871, and the present civil war, where he hounds on the prisoners of Sedan and Metz against Paris by special permission of Bismarck. Despite his versatility of talent and shiftiness of purpose, this man has his whole lifetime been wedded to the most fossil routine. It is self-evident that to him the deeper undercurrents of modern society remained forever hidden; but even the most palpable changes on its surface were abhorrent to a brain all the vitality of which had fled to the tongue. Thus he never tired of denouncing as a sacrilege any deviation from the old French protective system.[38] When a minister of Louis Philippe, he railed at railways as a wild chimera; and when in opposition under Louis Bonaparte, he branded as a profanation every attempt to reform the rotten French army system. Never in his long political career has he been guilty of a single— even the smallest—measure of any practical use. Thiers was consistent only in his greed for wealth and his hatred of the men that produce it. Having entered his first ministry under Louis Philippe poor as Job, he left it a millionaire. His last ministry under the same king (of the 1st of March, 1840) exposed him to public taunts of peculation in the Chamber of Deputies, to which he was content to reply by tears—a commodity he deals in as freely as Jules Favre, or any other crocodile. At Bordeaux his first measure for saving France from impending financial ruin was to endow himself with three millions a year, the first and the last word of the "Economical Republic," the vista of which he had opened to his Paris electors in 1869. One of his former colleagues of the Chamber of Deputies of 1830, himself a capitalist and, nevertheless, a devoted member of the Paris Commune, M. Beslay, lately addressed Thiers thus in a public placard: "The enslavement of labour by capital has always been the cornerstone of your policy, and from the very day you saw the Republic of Labour installed at the Hôtel de Ville, you have never ceased to cry out to France: 'These are criminals!'" A master in small state roguery, a virtuoso in perjury and treason, a craftsman in all the petty stratagems, cunning devices, and base perfidies of parliamentary party warfare; never scrupling, when out of office, to fan a revolution, and to stifle it in blood when at the helm of the state; with class prejudices standing him in the place of ideas, and vanity in the place of a heart; his private life as infamous as his public life is odious—even now, when playing the part of a French Sulla, he cannot help setting off the abomination of his deeds by the ridicule of his ostentation.

The capitulation of Paris, by surrendering to Prussia not only Paris, but all France, closed the long-continued intrigues of treason with the enemy, which the usurpers of the 4th September had begun, as Trochu himself said, on that very same day. On the other hand, it initiated the civil war they were now to wage, with the assistance of Prussia, against the republic and Paris. The trap was laid in the very terms of the capitulation. At that time above one-third of the territory was in the hands of the enemy, the capital was cut off from the provinces, all communications were disorganised. To elect under such circumstances a real representation of France was impossible, unless ample time were given for preparation. In view of this, the capitulation stipulated that a National Assembly must be elected within eight days; so that in many parts of France the news of the impending election arrived on its eve only. This assembly, moreover, was, by an express clause of the capitulation, to be elected for the sole purpose of deciding on peace or war, and, eventually, to conclude a treaty of peace. The population could not but feel that the terms of the armistice rendered the continuation of the war impossible, and that for sanctioning the peace imposed by Bismarck, the worst men in France were the best. But not content with these precautions, Thiers even before the secret of the armistice had been broached to Paris, set out for an electioneering tour through the provinces, there to galvanise back into life the Legitimist party, which now, along with the Orleanists, had to take the place of the then impossible Bonapartists. He was not afraid of them. Impossible as a government of modern France, and, therefore, contemptible as rivals, what party were more eligible as tools of counter-revolution than the party whose action, in the words of Thiers himself (Chamber of Deputies, 5th January, 1833), "had always been confined to the three resources of foreign invasion, civil war, and anarchy"? They verily believed in the advent of their long-expected retrospective millennium. There were the heels of foreign invasion trampling upon France; there was the downfall of an empire, and the captivity of a Bonaparte; and there they were themselves. The wheel of history had evidently rolled back to stop at the "Chambre introuvable" [39] of 1816. In the assemblies of the republic, 1848 to 1851, they had been represented by their educated and trained parliamentary champions; it was the rank-and-file of the party which now rushed in—all the Pourceaugnacs of France.

As soon as this Assembly of "Rurals" [40] had met at Bordeaux, Thiers made it clear to them that the peace preliminaries must be assented to at once, without even the honours of a parliamentary debate, as the only condition on which Prussia would permit them to open the war against the republic and Paris, its stronghold. The counter-revolution had, in fact, no time to lose. The Second Empire had more than doubled the national debt, and plunged all the large towns into heavy municipal debts. The war had fearfully swelled the liabilities, and mercilessly ravaged the resources of the nation. To complete the ruin, the Prussian Shylock was there with his bond for the keep of half a million of his soldiers on French soil, his indemnity of five milliards, and interest at 5 per cent on the unpaid instalments thereof. Who was to pay the bill? It was only by the violent overthrow of the republic that the appropriators of wealth could hope to shift on to the shoulders of its producers the cost of a war which they, the appropriators, had themselves originated. Thus, the immense ruin of France spurred on these patriotic representatives of land and capital, under the very eyes and patronage of the invader, to graft upon the foreign war a civil war—a slaveholders' rebellion.

There stood in the way of this conspiracy one great obstacle—Paris. To disarm Paris was the first condition of success. Paris was therefore summoned by Thiers to surrender its arms. Then Paris was exasperated by the frantic anti-republican demonstrations of the "Rural" Assembly and by Thiers' own equivocations about the legal status of the republic; by the threat to decapitate and decapitalise Paris; the appointment of Orleanist ambassadors; Dufaure's laws on over-due commercial bills and house rents, inflicting ruin on the commerce and industry of Paris; Pouyer-Quertier's tax of two centimes upon every copy of every imaginable publication; the sentences of death against Blanqui and Flourens; the suppression of the republican journals; the transfer of the National Assembly to Versailles; the renewal of the state of siege declared by Palikao, and expired on the 4th of September; the appointment of Vinoy, the *Décembriseur,* as governor of Paris—of Valentin, the imperialist *gendarme,* as its prefect of police—and of D'Aurelles de Paladine, the Jesuit general, as the commander-in-chief of its National Guard.

And now we have to address a question to M. Thiers and the men of national defence, his under-strappers. It is known that, through the agency of M. Pouyer-Quertier, his finance ministers, Thiers had contracted a loan of two milliards. Now, is it true or not—

1. That the business was so managed that a consideration of several hundred millions was secured for the private benefit of Thiers, Jules Favre, Ernest Picard, Pouyer-Quertier, and Jules Simon? and—

2. That no money was to be paid down until after the "pacification" of Paris?

At all events, there must have been something very pressing in the matter, for Thiers and Jules Favre, in the name of the majority of the Bordeaux Assembly, unblushingly solicited the immediate occupation of Paris by Prussian troops. Such, however, was not the game of Bismarck, as he sneeringly, and in public, told the admiring Frankfort philistines on his return to Germany.

II

Armed Paris was the only serious obstacle in the way of the counter-revolutionary conspiracy. Paris was, therefore, to be disarmed. On this point the Bordeaux Assembly was sincerity itself. If the roaring rant of its Rurals had not been audible enough, the surrender of Paris by Thiers to the tender mercies of the triumvirate of Vinoy the *Décembriseur,* Valentin the Bonapartist *gendarme,* and Aurelles de Paladine the Jesuit general, would have cut off even the last subterfuge of doubt. But while insultingly exhibiting the true purpose of the disarmament of Paris, the conspirators asked her to lay down her arms on a pretext which was the most glaring, the most barefaced of lies. The artillery of the Paris National Guard, said Thiers, belonged to the state, and to the state it must be returned. The fact was this: From the very day of the capitulation, by which Bismarck's prisoners had signed the surrender of France, but reserved to themselves a numerous bodyguard for the express purpose of cowing Paris, Paris stood on the watch. The National Guard reorganised themselves and intrusted their supreme control to a Central Committee elected by their whole body, save some fragments of the old Bonapartist formations. On the eve of the entrance of the Prussians into Paris, the Central Committee took measures for the removal to Montmartre, Belleville, and La Villette of the cannon and *mitrailleuses* treacherously abandoned by the *capitulards* in and about the very quarters the Prussians were to occupy. That artillery had been furnished by the subscriptions of the National Guard. As their private property, it was officially recognised in the capitulation of the 28th of January, and on that very title exempted from the general surrender, into the hands of the conqueror, of arms belonging to the government. And Thiers was so utterly destitute of even the flimsiest pretext for initiating the war against Paris, that he had to resort to the flagrant lie of the artillery of the National Guard being state property!

The seizure of her artillery was evidently but to serve as the preliminary to the general disarmament of Paris, and, therefore, of the Revolution of the 4th of September. But that revolution had become the legal status of France. The republic, its work, was recognised by the conqueror in the terms of the capitulation. After the capitulation, it was acknowledged by all the foreign powers, and in its name the National Assembly had been summoned. The Paris working men's revolution of the 4th of September was the only legal title of the National Assembly seated at Bordeaux, and of its executive. Without it, the National Assembly would at once have to give way to the *Corps Législatif* elected in 1869 by universal suffrage under French, not under Prussian, rule, and forcibly dispersed by the arm of the revolution. Thiers and his ticket-of-leave men would have had to capitulate for safe conducts signed by Louis Bonaparte, to save them from a voyage to Cayenne.[41] The National Assembly, with its power of attorney to settle the terms of peace with Prussia, was but an incident of that revolution, the true embodiment of which was still armed Paris, which had initiated it, undergone for it a five-months' siege, with its horrors of famine, and made her prolonged resistance, despite Trochu's plan, the basis of an obstinate war of defence in the provinces. And Paris was now either to lay down her arms at the insulting behest of the rebellious slaveholders of Bordeaux, and acknowledge that her Revolution of the 4th of September meant nothing but a simple transfer of power from Louis Bonapart to his royal rivals; or she had to stand forward as the self-sacrificing champion of France, whose salvation from ruin and whose regeneration were impossible without the revolutionary overthrow of the political and social conditions that had engendered the Second Empire, and, under its fostering care, matured into utter rottenness. Paris, emaciated by a five-months' famine, did not hesitate one moment. She heroically resolved to run all the hazards of a resistance against the French conspirators, even with Prussian cannon frowning upon her from her own forts. Still, in its abhorrence of the civil war into which Paris was to be goaded, the Central Committee continued to persist in a merely defensive attitude, despite the provocations of the Assembly, the usurpations of the Executive, and the menacing concentration of troops in and around Paris.

Thiers opened the civil war by sending Vinoy, at the head of a multitude of *sergents-de-ville* and some regiments of the line, upon a nocturnal expedition against Montmartre, there to seize, by surprise, the artillery of the National Guard. It is well known how this attempt broke down before the resistance of the National Guard and the fraternisation of the line with the people. Aurelles de Paladine had printed beforehand his bulletin of victory, and Thiers held ready the placards announcing his measures of *coup d'état*. Now these had to be replaced by Thiers' appeals, imparting his magnanimous resolve to leave the National Guard in the possession of their arms, with which, he said, he felt sure they would rally round the government against the rebels. Out of 300,000 National Guards only 300 responded to this summons to rally round little Thiers against themselves. The glorious working men's Revolution of the 18th March took undisputed sway of Paris. The Central Committee was its provisional government. Europe seemed, for a moment, to doubt whether its recent sensational performances of state and war had any reality in them or whether they were the dreams of a long bygone past.

From the 18th of March to the entrance of the Versailles troops into Paris, the proletarian revolution remained so free from the acts of violence in which the revolutions, and still more the counter-revolutions, of the "better classes" abound, that no facts were left to its opponents to cry out about, but the execution of Generals Lecomte and Clement Thomas, and the affair of the Place Vendôme.

One of the Bonapartist officers engaged in the nocturnal attempt against Montmartre, General Lecomte, had four times ordered the 81st line regiment to fire at an unarmed gathering in the Place Pigalle, and on their refusal fiercely insulted them. Instead of shooting women and children, his own men shot him. The inveterate habits acquired by the soldiery under the training of the enemies of the working class are, of course, not likely to change the very moment these soldiers change sides. The same men executed Clement Thomas.

"General" Clement Thomas, a malcontent ex-quartermaster-sergeant, had, in the latter times of Louis Philippe's reign, enlisted at the office of the republican newspaper *Le National,* there to serve in the double capacity of responsible man-of-straw (*gérant responsable*)[42] and of duelling bully to that very combative journal. After the Revolution of February, the men of the *National* having got into power, they metamorphosed this old quarter-master-sergeant into a general on the eve of the butchery of June, of which he, like Jules Favre, was one of the sinister plotters, and became one of the most dastardly executioners. Then he and his generalship disappeared for a long time, to again rise to the surface on the 1st November, 1870. The day before [43] the Government of Defence, caught at the Hôtel de Ville, had solemnly pledged their parole to Blanqui, Flourens, and other representatives of the working class, to abdicate their usurped power into the hands of a commune to be freely elected by Paris. Instead of keeping their word, they let loose on Paris the Bretons of Trochu, who now replaced the Corsicans of Bonaparte. General Tamisier alone, refusing to sully his name by such a breach of faith, resigned the commandership-in-chief of the National Guard, and in his place Clement Thomas for once became again a general. During the whole of his tenure of command, he made war, not upon the Prussians, but upon the Paris National Guard. He prevented their general armament, pitted the bourgeois battalions against the working men's battalions, weeded out the officers hostile to Trochu's "plan," and disbanded, under the stigma of cowardice, the very same proletarian battalions whose heroism has now astonished their most inveterate enemies. Clement Thomas felt quite proud of having reconquered his June preeminence as the personal enemy of the working class of Paris. Only a few days before the 18th of March, he laid before the War Minister, Leflô, a plan of his own for "finishing off *la fine fleur* [the

cream] of the Paris *canaille.*" After Vinoy's rout, he must needs
appear upon the scene of action in the quality of an amateur spy.
The Central Committee and the Paris working men were as much
responsible for the killing of Clement Thomas and Lecomte as the
Princess of Wales for the fate of the people crushed to death on
the day of her entrance into London.

The massacre of unarmed citizens in the Place Vendôme is a
myth which M. Thiers and the Rurals persistently ignored in the
Assembly, entrusting its propagation exclusively to the servants'
hall of European journalism. "The men of order," the reactionists
of Paris, trembled at the victory of the 18th of March. To them
it was the signal of popular retribution at last arriving. The ghosts
of the victims assassinated at their hands from the days of June
1848, down to the 22nd of January, 1871,[44] arose before their faces.
Their panic was their only punishment. Even the *sergents-de-ville,*
instead of being disarmed and locked up, as ought to have been
done, had the gates of Paris flung wide open for their safe retreat
to Versailles. The men of order were left not only unharmed, but
allowed to rally and quietly to seize more than one stronghold in
the very centre of Paris. This indulgence of the Central Committee
—this magnanimity of the armed working men—so strangely at
variance with the habits of the "Party of Order," the latter mis-
interpreted as mere symptoms of conscious weakness. Hence their
silly plan to try, under the cloak of an unarmed demonstration,
what Vinoy had failed to perform with his cannon and *mitrailleuses.* On the 22nd of March a riotous mob of swells started from
the quarters of luxury, all the *petits crevés* in their ranks, and at
their head the notorious familiars of the empire—the Heeckeren,
Coëtlogon, Henri de Pène, etc. Under the cowardly pretence of a
pacific demonstration, this rabble, secretly armed with the weapons
of the bravo, fell into marching order, ill treated and disarmed the
detached patrols and sentries of the National Guard they met with
on their progress, and, on debouching from the Rue de la Paix,
with the cry of "Down with the Central Committee! Down with
the assassins! The National Assembly for ever!" attempted to break
through the line drawn up there, and thus to carry by surprise

the headquarters of the National Guard in the Place Vendôme. In reply to their pistol-shots, the regular *sommations* (the French equivalent of the English Riot Act) were made, and, proving ineffective, fire was commanded by the general of the National Guard. One volley dispersed into wild flight the silly coxcombs, who expected that the mere exhibition of their "respectability" would have the same effect upon the Revolution of Paris as Joshua's trumpets upon the walls of Jericho. The runaways left behind them two National Guards killed, nine severely wounded (among them a member of the Central Committee), and the whole scene of their exploit strewn with revolvers, daggers, and sword-canes, in evidence of the "unarmed" character of their "pacific" demonstration. When, on the 13th of June, 1849, the National Guard made a really pacific demonstration in protest against the felonious assault of French troops upon Rome, Changarnier, then general of the Party of Order, was acclaimed by the National Assembly, and especially by M. Thiers, as the saviour of society, for having launched his troops from all sides upon these unarmed men, to shoot and sabre them down, and to trample them under their horses' feet. Paris, then, was placed under a state of siege. Dufaure hurried through the Assembly new laws of repression. New arrests, new proscriptions— a new reign of terror set in. But the lower orders manage these things otherwise. The Central Committee of 1871 simply ignored the heroes of the "pacific demonstration"; so much so, that only two days later they were enabled to muster under Admiral Saisset, for that *armed* demonstration, crowned by the famous stampede to Versailles. In their reluctance to continue the civil war opened by Thiers' burglarious attempt on Montmartre, the Central Committee made themselves, this time, guilty of a decisive mistake in not at once marching upon Versailles, then completely helpless, and thus putting an end to the conspiracies of Thiers and his Rurals. Instead of this, the Party of Order was again allowed to try its strength at the ballot box, on the 26th of March,[45] the day of the election of the Commune. Then, in the *mairies* of Paris, they exchanged bland words of conciliation with their too generous conquerors, muttering in their hearts solemn vows to exterminate them in due time.

Now, look at the reverse of the medal. Thiers opened his second campaign against Paris in the beginning of April. The first batch of Parisian prisoners brought into Versailles was subjected to revolting atrocities, while Ernest Picard, with his hands in his trousers' pockets, strolled about jeering them, and while Mesdames Thiers and Favre, in the midst of their ladies of honour (?) applauded, from the balcony, the outrages of the Versailles mob. The captured soldiers of the line were massacred in cold blood; our brave friend, General Duval, the iron-founder, was shot without any form of trial. Galifet, the kept man of his wife, so notorious for her shameless exhibitions at the orgies of the Second Empire, boasted in a proclamation of having commanded the murder of a small troop of National Guards, with their captain and lieutenant, surprised and disarmed by his Chasseurs. Vinoy, the runaway, was appointed by Thiers, Grand Cross of the Legion of Honour, for his general order to shoot down every soldier of the line taken in the ranks of the Federals. Desmarêt, the Gendarme, was decorated for the treacherous butcher-like chopping in pieces of the high-souled and chivalrous Flourens, who had saved the heads of the Government of Defence on the 31st of October, 1870. "The encouraging particulars" of his assassination were triumphantly expatiated upon by Thiers in the National Assembly. With the elated vanity of a parliamentary Tom Thumb, permitted to play the part of a Tamerlane, he denied the rebels against his littleness every right of civilised warfare, up to the right of neutrality for ambulances. Nothing more horrid than that monkey allowed for a time to give full fling to his tigerish instincts, as foreseen by Voltaire.

After the decree of the Commune of the 7th April ordering reprisals and declaring it to be its duty "to protect Paris against the cannibal exploits of the Versailles banditti, and to demand an eye for an eye, a tooth for a tooth," Thiers did not stop the barbarous treatment of prisoners, moreover insulting them in his bulletins as follows: "Never have more degraded countenances of a degraded democracy met the afflicted gazes of honest men,"—honest, like Thiers himself and his ministerial ticket-of-leave men. Still the shooting of prisoners was suspended for a time. Hardly, how-

ever, had Thiers and his Decembrist generals become aware that
the Communal decree of reprisals was but an empty threat, that
even their gendarme spies caught in Paris under the disguise of
National Guards, that even *sergents-de-ville,* taken with incendiary
shells upon them, were spared—when the wholesale shooting of
prisoners was resumed and carried on uninterruptedly to the end.
Houses to which National Guards had fled were surrounded by
gendarmes, inundated with petroleum (which here occurs for the
first time in this war), and then set fire to, the charred corpses
being afterwards brought out by the ambulance of the Press at the
Ternes. Four National Guards having surrendered to a troop of
mounted Chasseurs at Belle Epine, on the 25th of April, were
afterwards shot down, one after another, by the captain, a worthy
man of Gallifet's. One of his four victims, left for dead, Scheffer,
crawled back to the Parisian outposts, and deposed to this fact before a commission of the Commune. When Tolain interpellated
the War Minister upon the report of this commission, the Rurals
drowned his voice and forbade Leflô to answer. It would be an
insult to their "glorious" army to speak of its deeds. The flippant
tone in which Thiers' bulletins announced the bayoneting of the Federals surprised asleep at Moulin Saquet, and the wholesale fusillades
at Clamart shocked the nerves even of the not over-sensitive London
Times. But it would be ludicrous today to attempt recounting the
merely preliminary atrocities committed by the bombarders of Paris
and the fomenters of a slaveholders' rebellion protected by foreign
invasion. Amidst all these horrors, Thiers, forgetful of his parliamentary laments on the terrible responsibility weighing down his
dwarfish shoulders, boasts in his bulletins that *l'Assemblée siège
paisiblement* (the Assembly continues meeting in peace), and proves
by his constant carousals, now with Decembrist generals, now with
German princes, that his digestion is not troubled in the least, not
even by the ghosts of Lecomte and Clement Thomas.

III

On the dawn of the 18th of March, Paris arose to the thunder-burst of "Vive la Commune!" What is the Commune, that sphinx so tantalising to the bourgeois mind?

"The proletarians of Paris," said the Central Committee in its manifesto of the 18th March, "amidst the failures and treasons of the ruling classes, have understood that the hour has struck for them to save the situation by taking into their own hands the direction of public affairs.... They have understood that it is their imperious duty and their absolute right to render themselves mas-ters of their own destinies, by seizing upon the governmental power." But the working class cannot simply lay hold of the ready-made state machinery, and wield it for its own purposes.[46]

The centralised state power, with its ubiquitous organs of standing army, police, bureaucracy, clergy, and judicature—organs wrought after the plan of a systematic and hierarchic division of labour—originates from the days of absolute monarchy, serving nascent middle class society as a mighty weapon in its struggles against feudalism. Still, its development remained clogged by all manner of mediæval rubbish, seignorial rights, local privileges, municipal and guild monopolies and provincial constitutions. The gigantic broom of the French Revolution of the eighteenth century swept away all these relics of bygone times, thus clearing simul-taneously the social soil of its last hindrances to the superstructure of the modern state edifice raised under the First Empire, itself the offspring of the coalition wars [47] of old semi-feudal Europe against modern France. During the subsequent *régimes* the government, placed under parliamentary control—that is, under the direct con-trol of the propertied classes—became not only a hotbed of huge national debts and crushing taxes; with its irresistible allurements of place, pelf, and patronage, it became not only the bone of con-tention between the rival factions and adventurers of the ruling classes; but its political character changed simultaneously with the economic changes of society. At the same pace at which the progress of modern industry developed, widened, intensified the class antagonism between capital and labour, the state power assumed more and more the character of the national power of capital over labour, of a public force organised for social enslavement, of an engine of class despotism. After every revolution marking a progressive phase in the class struggle, the purely repressive character of the state power stands out in bolder and bolder relief. The Revolution of 1830, resulting in the transfer of government from the landlords to the capitalists, transferred it from the more remote to the more direct antagonists of the working men. The bourgeois republicans, who, in the name of the Revolution of February, took the state power, used it for the June massacres, in order to convince the working class that "social" republic meant the republic ensuring their social subjection, and in order to convince the royalist bulk of the bourgeois and landlord class that they might safely leave the cares and emoluments of government to the bourgeois "republicans." However, after their one heroic exploit of June, the bourgeois republicans had, from the front, to fall back to the rear of the "Party of Order"—a combination formed by all the rival fractions and factions of the appropriating class in their now openly declared antagonism to the producing classes. The proper form of their joint-stock government was the *parliamentary republic,* with Louis Bonaparte for its president. Theirs was a *régime* of avowed class terrorism and deliberate insult towards the "vile multitude." If the parliamentary republic, as M. Thiers said, "divided them [the different fractions of the ruling class] least," it opened an abyss between that class and the whole body of society outside their spare ranks. The restraints by which their own divisions had under former *régimes* still checked the state power, were removed by their union; and in view of the threatening upheaval of the proletariat, they now used that state power mercilessly and ostentatiously as the national war engine of capital against labour. In their uninterrupted crusade against the producing masses they were, however, bound not only to invest the executive with continually increased powers of repression, but at the same time to divest their own parliamentary stronghold—the National Assembly—one by one, of all its own means of defence against the Executive. The Executive, in the person of Louis Bonaparte, turned them out. The natural offspring of the "Party of Order" republic was the Second Empire.

The empire, with the *coup d'état* for its certificate of birth, universal suffrage for its sanction, and the sword for its sceptre, professed to rest upon the peasantry, the large mass of producers not directly involved in the struggle of capital and labour. It professed to save the working class by breaking down parliamentarism, and, with it, the undisguised subserviency of government to the propertied classes. It professed to save the propertied classes by upholding their economic supremacy over the working class; and, finally, it professed to unite all classes by reviving for all the chimera of national glory. In reality, it was the only form of government possible at a time when the bourgeoisie had already lost, and the working class had not yet acquired, the faculty of ruling the nation. It was acclaimed throughout the world as the saviour of society. Under its sway, bourgeois society, freed from political cares, attained a development unexpected even by itself. Its industry and commerce expanded to colossal dimensions; financial swindling celebrated cosmopolitan orgies; the misery of the masses was set off by a shameless display of gorgeous, meretricious and debased luxury. The state power, apparently soaring high above society, was at the same time itself the greatest scandal of that society and the very hotbed of all its corruptions. Its own rottenness, and the rottenness of the society it had saved, were laid bare by the bayonet of Prussia, herself eagerly bent upon transferring the supreme seat of that *régime* from Paris to Berlin. Imperialism [48] is, at the same time, the most prostitute and the ultimate form of the state power which nascent middle class society had commenced to elaborate as a means of its own emancipation from feudalism, and which full-grown bourgeois society had finally transformed into a means for the enslavement of labour by capital.

The direct antithesis to the empire was the Commune. The cry of "social republic" with which the Revolution of February was ushered in by the Paris proletariat, did but express a vague aspiration after a republic that was not only to supersede the monarchical form of class rule, but class rule itself. The Commune was the positive form of that republic.

Paris, the central seat of the old governmental power, and, at the same time, the social stronghold of the French working class, had risen in arms against the attempt of Thiers and the Rurals to restore and perpetuate that old governmental power bequeathed to them by the empire. Paris could resist only because, in consequence of the siege, it had got rid of the army, and replaced it by a National Guard, the bulk of which consisted of working men. This fact was now to be transformed into an institution. The first decree of the Commune, therefore, was the suppression of the standing army, and the substitution for it of the armed people.

The Commune was formed of the municipal councillors, chosen by universal suffrage in the various wards of the town, responsible and revocable at short terms. The majority of its members were naturally working men, or acknowledged representatives of the working class. The Commune was to be a working, not a parliamentary body, executive and legislative at the same time.[49] Instead of continuing to be the agent of the Central Government, the police was at once stripped of its political attributes, and turned into the responsible and at all times revocable agent of the Commune. So were the officials of all other branches of the administration. From the members of the Commune downwards, the public service had to be done at *workmen's wages*. The vested interests and the representation allowances of the high dignitaries of state disappeared along with the high dignitaries themselves. Public functions ceased to be the private property of the tools of the Central Government. Not only municipal administration, but the whole initiative hitherto exercised by the state was laid into the hands of the Commune.

Having once got rid of the standing army and the police, the physical force elements of the old government, the Commune was anxious to break the spiritual force of repression, the "parson-power," by the disestablishment and disendowment of all churches as proprietary bodies. The priests were sent back to the recesses of private life, there to feed upon the alms of the faithful in imitation of their predecessors, the apostles. The whole of the educational institutions were opened to the people gratuitously, and at the same time cleared of all interference of church and state. Thus, not only was education made accessible to all, but science itself freed from the fetters which class prejudice and governmental force had imposed upon it.

The judicial functionaries were to be divested of that sham independence which had but served to mask their abject subserviency to all succeeding governments to which, in turn, they had taken, and broken, the oaths of allegiance. Like the rest of public servants, magistrates and judges were to be elective, responsible and revocable.

The Paris Commune was, of course, to serve as a model to all the great industrial centres of France. The communal *régime* once established in Paris and the secondary centres, the old centralised government would in the provinces, too, have to give way to the self-government of the producers. In a rough sketch of national organisation which the Commune had no time to develop, it states clearly that the Commune was to be the political form of even the smallest country hamlet, and that in the rural districts the standing army was to be replaced by a national militia, with an extremely short term of service. The rural communes of every district were to administer their common affairs by an assembly of delegates in the central town, and these district assemblies were again to send deputies to the National Delegation in Paris, each delegate to be at any time revocable and bound by the *mandat imperatif* (formal instructions) of his constituents. The few but important functions which still would remain for a central government were not to be suppressed, as has been intentionally misstated, but were to be discharged by Communal and therefore strictly responsible agents. The unity of the nation was not to be broken, but, on the contrary, to be organised by the Communal Constitution, and to become a reality by the destruction of the state power which claimed to be the embodiment of that unity independent of, and superior to, the nation itself, from which it was but a parasitic excrescence. While the merely repressive organs of the old governmental power were to be amputated, its legitimate functions were to be wrested from an authority usurping pre-eminence over society itself, and restored

to the responsible agents of society. Instead of deciding once in
three or six years which member of the ruling class was to misrepresent the people in Parliament,[50] universal suffrage was to serve
the people, constituted in Communes, as individual suffrage serves
every other employer in the search for the workmen and managers
in his business. And it is well known that companies, like individuals, in matters of real business generally know how to put the
right man in the right place, and, if they for once make a mistake,
to redress it promptly. On the other hand, nothing could be more
foreign to the spirit of the Commune than to supersede universal
suffrage by hierarchic investiture.

It is generally the fate of completely new historical creations to
be mistaken for the counterpart of older and even defunct forms
of social life, to which they may bear a certain likeness. Thus, this
new Commune, which breaks the modern state power, has been
mistaken for a reproduction of the mediæval Communes, which
first preceded, and afterwards became the substratum of, that very
state power.—The Communal Constitution has been mistaken for
an attempt to break up into a federation of small states, as dreamt
of by Montesquieu and the Girondins,[51] that unity of great nations
which, if originally brought about by political force, has now become a powerful coefficient of social production.—The antagonism
of the Commune against the state power has been mistaken for an
exaggerated form of the ancient struggle against over-centralisation.
Peculiar historical circumstances may have prevented the classical
development, as in France, of the bourgeois form of government,
and may have allowed, as in England, to complete the great central
state organs by corrupt vestries, jobbing councillors, and ferocious
poor-law guardians in the towns, and virtually hereditary magistrates in the counties. The Communal Constitution would have
restored to the social body all the forces hitherto absorbed by the
state parasite feeding upon, and clogging the free movement of,
society. By this one act it would have initiated the regeneration of
France. The provincial French middle class saw in the Commune
an attempt to restore the sway their order had held over the country under Louis Philippe, and which, under Louis Napoleon, was

supplanted by the pretended rule of the country over the towns. In reality, the Communal Constitution brought the rural producers under the intellectual lead of the central towns of their districts, and there secured to them, in the working men, the natural trustees of their interests. The very existence of the Commune involved, as a matter of course, local municipal liberty, but no longer as a check upon the now superseded state power. It could only enter into the head of a Bismarck, who, when not engaged on his intrigues of blood and iron, always likes to resume his old trade, so befitting his mental calibre, of contributor to *Kladderadatsch* (the Berlin *Punch*), it could only enter into such a head to ascribe to the Paris Commune aspirations after that caricature of the old French municipal organisation of 1791, the Prussian municipal constitution which degrades the town governments to mere secondary wheels in the police machinery of the Prussian state. The Commune made that catchword of bourgeois revolutions, cheap government, a reality by destroying the two greatest sources of expenditure—the standing army and state functionarism. Its very existence presupposed the non-existence of monarchy, which, in Europe at least, is the normal incumbrance and indispensable cloak of class rule. It supplied the republic with the basis of really democratic institutions. But neither cheap government nor the "true republic" was its ultimate aim; they were its mere concomitants.

The multiplicity of interpretations to which the Commune has been subjected, and the multiplicity of interests which construed it in their favour, show that it was a thoroughly expansive political form, while all previous forms of government had been emphatically repressive. Its true secret was this. It was essentially a working class government, the produce of the struggle of the producing against the appropriating class, the political form at last discovered under which to work out the economical emancipation of labour.[52]

Except on this last condition, the Communal Constitution would have been an impossibility and a delusion. The political rule of the producer cannot co-exist with the perpetuation of his social slavery. The Commune was therefore to serve as a lever for uprooting the economical foundations upon which rests the existence of classes, and therefore of class rule. With labour emancipated, every man becomes a working man, and productive labour ceases to be a class attribute.

It is a strange fact. In spite of all the tall talk and all the immense literature, for the last sixty years, about emancipation of labour, no sooner do the working men anywhere take the subject into their own hands with a will, than uprises at once all the apologetic phraseology of the mouthpieces of present society with its two poles of capital and wages-slavery (the landlord now is but the sleeping partner of the capitalist), as if capitalist society was still in its purest state of virgin innocence, with its antagonisms still undeveloped, with its delusions still unexploded, with its prostitute realities not yet laid bare. The Commune, they exclaim, intends to abolish property, the basis of all civilisation! Yes, gentlemen, the Commune intended to abolish that class property which makes the labour of the many the wealth of the few. It aimed at the expropriation of the expropriators. It wanted to make individual property a truth by transforming the means of production, land and capital, now chiefly the means of enslaving and exploiting labour, into mere instruments of free and associated labour. But this is communism, "impossible" communism! Why, those members of the ruling classes who are intelligent enough to perceive the impossibility of continuing the present system—and they are many—have become the obtrusive and full-mouthed apostles of co-operative production. If co-operative production is not to remain a sham and a snare; if it is to supersede the capitalist system; if united co-operative societies are to regulate national production upon a common plan, thus taking it under their own control, and putting an end to the constant anarchy and periodical convulsions which are the fatality of capitalist production—what else, gentlemen, would it be but communism, "possible" communism?

The working class did not expect miracles from the Commune. They have no ready-made utopias to introduce *par decret du peuple*. They know that in order to work out their own emancipation, and along with it that higher form to which present society is irresistibly tending by its own economical agencies, they will have to pass through long struggles, through a series of historic processes, transforming circumstances and men. They have no ideals to realise, but to set free the elements of the new society with which old collapsing bourgeois society itself is pregnant. In the full consciousness of their historic mission, and with the heroic resolve to act up to it, the working class can afford to smile at the coarse invective of the gentlemen's gentlemen with the pen and inkhorn, and at the didactic patronage of well-wishing bourgeois-doctrinaires, pouring forth their ignorant platitudes and sectarian crotchets in the oracular tone of scientific infallibility.

When the Paris Commune took the management of the revolution in its own hands; when plain working men for the first time dared to infringe upon the governmental privilege of their "natural superiors," and, under circumstances of unexampled difficulty, performed their work modestly, conscientiously, and efficiently—performed it at salaries the highest of which barely amounted to one-fifth of what, according to high scientific authority is the minimum required for a secretary to a certain metropolitan school-board—the old world writhed in convulsions of rage at the sight of the Red Flag, the symbol of the Republic of Labour, floating over the Hôtel de Ville.

And yet, this was the first revolution in which the working class was openly acknowledged as the only class capable of social initiative, even by the great bulk of the Paris middle class—shopkeepers, tradesmen, merchants—the wealthy capitalist alone excepted. The Commune had saved them [53] by a sagacious settlement of that ever recurring cause of dispute among the middle class themselves—the debtor and creditor accounts. The same portion of the middle class, after they had assisted in putting down the working men's insurrection of June 1848, had been at once unceremoniously sacrificed to their creditors by the then Constituent Assembly. But this was not their only motive for now rallying round the working class. They felt there was but one alternative—the Commune, or the empire—under whatever name it might reappear. The empire had ruined them economically by the havoc it made of public wealth, by the wholesale financial swindling it fostered, by the props it lent

to the artificially accelerated centralisation of capital, and the concomitant expropriation of their own ranks. It had suppressed them
politically, it had shocked them morally by its orgies, it had insulted
their Voltairianism [54] by handing over the education of their children to the *frères Ignorantins,* it had revolted their national feeling
as Frenchmen by precipitating them headlong into a war which
left only one equivalent for the ruins it made—the disappearance
of the empire. In fact, after the exodus from Paris of the high
Bonapartist and capitalist *bôhème,* the true middle class Party of
Order came out in the shape of the *"Union Républicaine,"* enrolling
themselves under the colours of the Commune and defending it
against the wilful misconstruction of Thiers. Whether the gratitude
of this great body of the middle class will stand the present severe
trial, time must show.

The Commune was perfectly right in telling the peasants that
"its victory was their only hope." Of all the lies hatched at Versailles
and re-echoed by the glorious European penny-a-liner, one of the
most tremendous was that the Rurals represented the French peasantry. Think only of the love of the French peasant for the men
to whom, after 1815, he had to pay the milliard of indemnity! [55]
In the eyes of the French peasant, the very existence of a great
landed proprietor is in itself an encroachment on his conquests of
1789. The bourgeois, in 1848, had burdened his plot of land with
the additional tax of forty-five cents,[56] in the franc; but then he
did so in the name of the revolution; while now he had fomented
a civil war against the revolution, to shift on to the peasant's
shoulders the chief load of the five milliards of indemnity to be
paid to the Prussian. The Commune, on the other hand, in one of
its first proclamations, declared that the true originators of the war
would be made to pay its cost. The Commune would have delivered
the peasant of the blood tax—would have given him a cheap government—transformed his present blood-suckers, the notary, advo-
cate, executor, and other judicial vampires, into salaried communal
agents, elected by, and responsible to, himself. It would have freed
him of the tyranny of the *garde champêtre,* the gendarme, and the
prefect; would have put enlightenment by the schoolmaster in the

place of stultification by the priest. And the French peasant is, above all, a man of reckoning. He would find it extremely reasonable that the pay of the priest, instead of being extorted by the tax-gatherer, should only depend upon the spontaneous action of the parishioners' religious instincts. Such were the great immediate boons which the rule of the Commune—and that rule alone—held out to the French peasantry. It is, therefore, quite superfluous here to expatiate upon the more complicated but vital problems which the Commune alone was able, and at the same time compelled, to solve in favour of the peasant, *viz.,* the hypothecary debt, lying like an incubus upon his parcel of soil, the *prolétariat foncier* (the rural proletariat), daily growing upon it, and his expropriation from it enforced, at a more and more rapid rate, by the very development of modern agriculture and the competition of capitalist farming.

The French peasant had elected Louis Bonaparte president of the republic; but the Party of Order [57] created the empire. What the French peasant really wants he commenced to show in 1849 and 1850, by opposing his *maire* to the government's prefect, his school-master to the government's priest, and himself to the government's gendarme. All the laws made by the Party of Order in January and February 1850 were avowed measures of repression against the peasant. The peasant was a Bonapartist, because the Great Revolution, with all its benefits to him, was, in his eyes, personified in Napoleon. This delusion, rapidly breaking down under the Second Empire (and in its very nature hostile to the Rurals), this prejudice of the past, how could it have withstood the appeal of the Commune to the living interests and urgent wants of the peasantry?

The Rurals—this was, in fact, their chief apprehension—knew that three months' free communication of Communal Paris with the provinces would bring about a general rising of the peasants, and hence their anxiety to establish a police blockade around Paris, so as to stop the spread of the rinderpest.

If the Commune was thus the true representative of all the healthy elements of French society, and therefore the truly national government, it was, at the same time, as a working men's government, as the bold champion of the emancipation of labour, emphatically international. Within sight of the Prussian army, that had annexed to Germany two French provinces,[58] the Commune annexed to France the working people all over the world.

The Second Empire had been the jubilee of cosmopolitan blackleggism, the rakes of all countries rushing in at its call for a share in its orgies and in the plunder of the French people. Even at this moment the right hand of Thiers is Ganessco, the foul Wallachian, and his left hand is Markovsky, the Russian spy. The Commune admitted all foreigners to the honour of dying for an immortal cause. Between the foreign war lost by their treason, and the civil war fomented by their conspiracy with the foreign invader, the bourgeoisie had found the time to display their patriotism by organising police hunts upon the Germans in France. The Commune made a German working man its Minister of Labour. Thiers, the bourgeoisie, the Second Empire, had continually deluded Poland by loud professions of sympathy, while in reality betraying her to, and doing the dirty work of, Russia. The Commune honoured the heroic sons of Poland by placing them at the head of the defenders of Paris. And, to broadly mark the new era of history it was conscious of initiating, under the eyes of the conquering Prussians on the one side, and of the Bonapartist army, led by Bonapartist generals, on the other, the Commune pulled down that colossal symbol of martial glory, the Vendôme Column.

The great social measure of the Commune was its own working existence. Its special measures could but betoken the tendency of a government of the people by the people. Such were the abolition of the nightwork of journeymen bakers; the prohibition, under penalty, of the employers' practice to reduce wages by levying upon their workpeople fines under manifold pretexts—a process in which the employer combines in his own person the parts of legislator, judge, and executor, and filches the money to boot. Another measure of this class was the surrender to associations of workmen, under reserve of compensation, of all closed workshops and factories, no matter whether the respective capitalists had absconded or preferred to strike work.

The financial measures of the Commune, remarkable for their

sagacity and moderation, could only be such as were compatible with the state of a besieged town. Considering the colossal robberies committed upon the city of Paris by the great financial companies and contractors, under the protection of Haussmann,[59] the Commune would have had an incomparably better title to confiscate their property than Louis Napoleon had against the Orleans family. The Hohenzollern and the English oligarchs, who both have derived a good deal of their estates from church plunder, were, of course, greatly shocked at the Commune clearing but 8,000 *f.* out of secularisation.

While the Versailles government, as soon as it had recovered some spirit and strength, used the most violent means against the Commune; while it put down the free expression of opinion all over France, even to the forbidding of meetings of delegates from the large towns; while it subjected Versailles and the rest of France to an espionage far surpassing that of the Second Empire; while it burned by its gendarme inquisitors all papers printed at Paris, and sifted all correspondence from and to Paris; while in the National Assembly the most timid attempts to put in a word for Paris were howled down in a manner unknown even to the *Chambre introuvable* of 1816; with the savage warfare of Versailles outside, and its attempts at corruption and conspiracy inside Paris— would the Commune not have shamefully betrayed its trust by affecting to keep up all the decencies and appearances of liberalism as in a time of profound peace? Had the government of the Commune been akin to that of M. Thiers, there would have been no more occasion to suppress Party of Order papers at Paris than there was to suppress Communal papers at Versailles.

It was irritating indeed to the Rurals that at the very same time they declared the return to the church to be the only means of salvation for France, the infidel Commune unearthed the peculiar mysteries of the Picpus nunnery, and of the Church of St. Laurent.[60] It was a satire upon M. Thiers that, while he showered grand crosses upon the Bonapartist generals in acknowledgment of their mastery in losing battles, signing capitulations, and turning cigarettes at Wilhelmshöhe, the Commune dismissed and arrested its generals whenever they were suspected of neglecting their duties. The expulsion from, and arrest by, the Commune of one of its members who had slipped in under a false name, and had undergone at Lyons six days' imprisonment for simple bankruptcy, was it not a deliberate insult hurled at the forger, Jules Favre, then still the foreign minister of France, still selling France to Bismarck, and still dictating his orders to that paragon government of Belgium? But indeed the Commune did not pretend to infallibility, the invariable attribute of all governments of the old stamp. It published its doings and sayings, it initiated the public into all its shortcomings.

In every revolution there intrude, at the side of its true agents, men of a different stamp; some of them survivors of and devotees to past revolutions, without insight into the present movement, but preserving popular influence by their known honesty and courage, or by the sheer force of tradition; others mere brawlers, who, by dint of repeating year after year the same set of stereotyped declamations against the government of the day, have sneaked into the reputation of revolutionists of the first water. After the 18th of March, some such men did also turn up, and in some cases contrived to play pre-eminent parts. As far as their power went, they hampered the real action of the working class, exactly as men of that sort have hampered the full development of every previous revolution. They are an unavoidable evil: with time they are shaken off; but time was not allowed to the Commune.

Wonderful, indeed, was the change the Commune had wrought in Paris! No longer any trace of the meretricious Paris of the Second Empire! No longer was Paris the rendezvous of British landlords, Irish absentees,[61] American ex-slaveholders and shoddy men, Russian ex-serfowners, and Wallachian boyards. No more corpses at the morgue, no nocturnal burglaries, scarcely any robberies; in fact, for the first time since the days of February 1848, the streets of Paris were safe, and that without any police of any kind. "We," said a member of the Commune, "hear no longer of assassination, theft and personal assault; it seems indeed as if the police had dragged along with it to Versailles all its Conservative

friends." The *cocottes* had refound the scent of their protectors—
the absconding men of family, religion, and, above all, of property.
In their stead, the real women of Paris showed again at the surface
—heroic, noble, and devoted, like the women of antiquity. Working,
thinking, fighting, bleeding Paris—almost forgetful, in its incuba-
tion of a new society, of the cannibals at its gates—radiant in the
enthusiasm of its historic initiative!

Opposed to this new world at Paris, behold the old world at
Versailles—that assembly of the ghouls of all defunct *régimes,* Legitimists and Orleanists, eager to feed upon the carcass of the nation
—with a tail of antediluvian republicans, sanctioning, by their presence in the Assembly, the slaveholders' rebellion, relying for the
maintenance of their parliamentary republic upon the vanity of
the senile mountebank at its head, and caricaturing 1789 by holding
their ghastly meetings in the *Jeu de Paume.*[62] There it was, this
Assembly, the representative of everything dead in France, propped
up to the semblance of life by nothing but the swords of the generals
of Louis Bonaparte. Paris all truth, Versailles all lie; and that lie
vented through the mouth of Thiers.

Thiers tells a deputation of the mayors of the Seine-et-Oise—
"You may rely upon my word, which I have *never* broken!" He
tells the Assembly itself that "it was the most freely elected and
most liberal Assembly France ever possessed"; he tells his motley
soldiery that it was "the admiration of the world, and the finest
army France ever possessed"; he tells the provinces that the bombardment of Paris by him was a myth: "If some cannon-shots have
been fired, it is not the deed of the army of Versailles, but of some
insurgents trying to make believe that they are fighting, while they
dare not show their faces." He again tells the provinces that "the
artillery of Versailles does not bombard Paris, but only cannonades
it." He tells the Archbishop of Paris that the pretended executions
and reprisals (!) attributed to the Versailles troops were all moon-
shine. He tells Paris that he was only anxious "to free it from the
hideous tyrants who oppress it," and that, in fact, the Paris of the
Commune was "but a handful of criminals."

The Paris of M. Thiers was not the real Paris of the "vile

multitude," but a phantom Paris, the Paris of the *francs-fileurs,* the
Paris of the Boulevards, male and female—the rich, the capitalist,
the gilded, the idle Paris, now thronging with its lackeys, its black-
legs, its literary *bôhème,* and its *cocottes* at Versailles, Saint-Denis,
Rueil, and Saint-Germain; considering the civil war but an agree-
able diversion, eyeing the battle going on through telescopes, count-
ing the rounds of cannon, and swearing by their own honour and
that of their prostitutes, that the performance was far better got
up than it used to be at the Porte St. Martin. The men who fell
were really dead; the cries of the wounded were cries in good
earnest; and, besides, the whole thing was so intensely historical.

This is the Paris of M. Thiers, as the emigration of Coblenz [63]
was the France of M. de Calonne.[64]

IV

The first attempt of the slaveholders' conspiracy to put down
Paris by getting the Prussians to occupy it was frustrated by Bismarck's refusal. The second attempt, that of the 18th of March,
ended in the rout of the army and the flight to Versailles of the
government, which ordered the whole administration to break up
and follow in its track. By the semblance of peace negotiations
with Paris, Thiers found the time to prepare for war against it.
But where to find an army? The remnants of the line regiments
were weak in number and unsafe in character. His urgent appeal
to the provinces to succour Versailles, by their National Guards
and volunteers, met with a flat refusal. Brittany alone furnished
a handful of *Chouans* fighting under a white flag, every one of
them wearing on his breast the heart of Jesus in white cloth, and
shouting *"Vive le Roi!"* (Long live the King!) Thiers was, therefore, compelled to collect, in hot haste, a motley crew, composed
of sailors, marines, Pontifical Zouaves, Valentin's gendarmes, and
Pietri's *sergents-de-ville* and *mouchards.* This army, however, would
have been ridiculously ineffective without the instalments of imperialist war prisoners, which Bismarck granted in numbers just
sufficient to keep the civil war agoing, and keep the Versailles

government in abject dependence on Prussia. During the war itself, the Versailles police had to look after the Versailles army, while the gendarmes had to drag it on by exposing themselves at all posts of danger. The forts which fell were not taken, but bought. The heroism of the Federals convinced Thiers that the resistance of Paris was not to be broken by his own strategic genius and the bayonets at his disposal.

Meanwhile, his relations with the provinces became more and more difficult. Not one single address of approval came in to gladden Thiers and his Rurals. Quite the contrary. Deputations and addresses demanding, in a tone anything but respectful, conciliation with Paris on the basis of the unequivocal recognition of the republic, the acknowledgment of the Communal liberties, and the dissolution of the National Assembly, whose mandate was extinct, poured in from all sides, and in such numbers that Dufaure, Thiers' Minister of Justice, in his circular of April 23 to the public prosecutors, commanded them to treat "the cry of conciliation" as a crime! In regard, however, of the hopeless prospect held out by his campaign, Thiers resolved to shift his tactics by ordering, all over the country, municipal elections to take place on the 30th of April, on the basis of the new municipal law dictated by himself to the National Assembly. What with the intrigues of his prefects, what with police intimidation, he felt quite sanguine of imparting, by the verdict of the provinces, to the National Assembly that moral power it had never possessed, and of getting at last from the provinces the physical force required for the conquest of Paris.

His banditti-warfare against Paris, exalted in his own bulletins, and the attempts of his ministers at the establishment, throughout France, of a reign of terror, Thiers was from the beginning anxious to accompany with a little by-play of conciliation, which had to serve more than one purpose. It was to dupe the provinces, to inveigle the middle class element in Paris, and, above all, to afford the professed republicans in the National Assembly the opportunity of hiding their treason against Paris behind their faith in Thiers. On the 21st of March, when still without an army, he had declared to the Assembly: "Come what may, I will not send an army to

Paris." On the 27th March he rose again: "I have found the republic
an accomplished fact, and I am firmly resolved to maintain it." In
reality, he put down the revolution at Lyons and Marseilles [65] in
the name of the republic, while the roars of his Rurals drowned
the very mention of its name at Versailles. After this exploit, he
toned down the "accomplished fact" into an hypothetical fact. The
Orleans princes, whom he had cautiously warned off Bordeaux,
were now, in flagrant breach of the law, permitted to intrigue at
Dreux. The concessions held out by Thiers in his interminable
interviews with the delegates from Paris and the provinces, although
constantly varied in tone and colour, according to time and circumstances, did in fact never come to more than the prospective restric-
tion of revenge to the "handful of criminals implicated in the
murder of Lecomte and Clement Thomas," on the well-understood
premise that Paris and France were unreservedly to accept M.
Thiers himself as the best of possible Republics, as he, in 1830, had
done with Louis Philippe. Even these concessions he not only took
care to render doubtful by the official comments put upon them in
the Assembly through his ministers. He had his Dufaure to act.
Dufaure, this old Orleanist lawyer, had always been the justiciary
of the state of siege, as now in 1871, under Thiers, so in 1839 under
Louis Philippe, and in 1849 under Louis Bonaparte's presidency.
While out of office he made a fortune by pleading for the Paris
capitalists, and made political capital by pleading against the laws
he had himself originated. He now hurried through the National
Assembly not only a set of repressive laws which were, after the
fall of Paris, to extirpate the last remnants of republican liberty in
France; he foreshadowed the fate of Paris by abridging the, for
him, too slow procedure of courts-martial, and by a new-fangled,
Draconic code of deportation. The Revolution of 1848, abolishing
the penalty of death for political crimes, had replaced it by deportation. Louis Bonaparte did not dare, at least not in theory, to re-
establish the regime of the guillotine. The Rural Assembly, not
yet bold enough even to hint that the Parisians were not rebels,
but assassins, had therefore to confine its prospective vengeance
against Paris to Dufaure's new code of deportation. Under all these

circumstances Thiers himself could not have gone on with his comedy of conciliation, had it not, as he intended it to do, drawn forth shrieks of rage from the Rurals, whose ruminating mind did neither understand the play, nor its necessities of hypocrisy, tergiversation, and procrastination.

In sight of the impending municipal elections of the 30th April, Thiers enacted one of his great conciliation scenes on the 27th April. Amidst a flood of sentimental rhetoric, he exclaimed from the tribune of the Assembly:

"There exists no conspiracy against the republic but that of Paris, which compels us to shed French blood. I repeat it again and again. Let those impious arms fall from the hands which hold them, and chastisement will be arrested at once by an act of peace excluding only the small number of criminals."

To the violent interruption of the Rurals he replied:

"Gentlemen, tell me, I implore you, am I wrong? Do you really regret that I could have stated the truth that the criminals are only a handful? Is it not fortunate in the midst of our misfortunes that those who have been capable to shed the blood of Clement Thomas and General Lecomte are but rare exceptions?"

France, however, turned a deaf ear to what Thiers flattered himself to be a parliamentary siren's song. Out of 700,000 municipal councillors returned by the 35,000 communes still left to France, the united Legitimists, Orleanists, and Bonapartists did not carry 8,000. The supplementary elections which followed were still more decidedly hostile. Thus, instead of getting from the provinces the badly-needed physical force, the National Assembly lost even its last claim to moral force, that of being the expression of the universal suffrage of the country. To complete the discomfiture, the newly-chosen municipal councils of all the cities of France openly threatened the usurping Assembly at Versailles with a counter assembly at Bordeaux.

Then the long-expected moment of decisive action had at last come for Bismarck. He peremptorily summoned Thiers to send to Frankfort plenipotentiaries for the definitive settlement of peace. In humble obedience to the call of his master, Thiers hastened to despatch his trusty Jules Favre, backed by Pouyer-Quertier. Pouyer-Quertier, an "eminent" Rouen cotton-spinner, a fervent and even servile partisan of the Second Empire, had never found any fault with it save its commercial treaty with England,[66] prejudicial to his own shop-interest. Hardly installed at Bordeaux as Thiers' Minister of Finance, he denounced that "unholy" treaty, hinted at its near abrogation, and had even the effrontery to try, although in vain (having counted without Bismarck), the immediate enforcement of the old protective duties against Alsace, where, he said, no previous international treaties stood in the way. This man who considered counter-revolution as a means to put down wages at Rouen, and the surrender of French provinces as a means to bring up the price of his wares in France, was he not *the one* predestined to be picked out by Thiers as the helpmate of Jules Favre in his last and crowning treason?

On the arrival at Frankfort of this exquisite pair of plenipotentiaries, bully Bismarck at once met them with the imperious alternative: Either the restoration of the empire or the unconditional acceptance of my own peace terms! These terms included a shortening of the intervals in which the war indemnity was to be paid and the continued occupation of the Paris forts by Prussian troops until Bismarck should feel satisfied with the state of things in France; Prussia thus being recognised as the supreme arbiter in internal French politics! In return for this he offered to let loose, for the extermination of Paris, the captive Bonapartist army, and to lend them the direct assistance of Emperor William's troops. He pledged his good faith by making payment of the first instalment of the indemnity dependent on the "pacification" of Paris. Such a bait was, of course, eagerly swallowed by Thiers and his plenipotentiaries. They signed the treaty of peace on the 10th of May and had it endorsed by the Versailles Assembly on the 18th.

In the interval between the conclusion of peace and the arrival of the Bonapartist prisoners, Thiers felt the more bound to resume his comedy of conciliation, as his republican tools stood in sore need of a pretext for blinking their eyes at the preparations for the carnage of Paris. As late as the 8th May he replied to a deputation of middle class conciliators—

"Whenever the insurgents will make up their minds for capitulation, the gates of Paris shall be flung wide open during a week for all except the murderers of Generals Clement Thomas and Lecomte."

A few days afterwards, when violently interpellated on these promises by the Rurals, he refused to enter into any explanations; not, however, without giving them this significant hint:

"I tell you there are impatient men amongst you, men who are in too great a hurry. They must have another eight days; at the end of these eight days there will be no more danger, and the task will be proportionate to their courage and to their capacities."

As soon as MacMahon was able to assure him that he could shortly enter Paris, Thiers declared to the Assembly that "he would enter Paris with the *laws* in his hands, and demand a full expiation from the wretches who had sacrificed the lives of soldiers and destroyed public monuments." As the moment of decision drew near he said—to the Assembly, "I shall be pitiless!"—to Paris, that it was doomed; and to his Bonapartist banditti, that they had state licence to wreak vengeance upon Paris to their hearts' content. At last, when treachery had opened the gates of Paris to General Douai, on the 21st May, Thiers, on the 22nd, revealed to the Rurals the "goal" of his conciliation comedy, which they had so obstinately persisted in not understanding. "I told you a few days ago that we were approaching *our goal;* today I come to tell you *the* goal is reached. The victory of order, justice and civilisation is at last won!"

So it was. The civilisation and justice of bourgeois order comes out in its lurid light whenever the slaves and drudges of that order rise against their masters. Then this civilisation and justice stand forth as undisguised savagery and lawless revenge. Each new crisis in the class struggle between the appropriator and the producer brings out this fact more glaringly. Even the atrocities of the bourgeois in June 1848 vanish before the ineffable infamy of 1871. The self-sacrificing heroism with which the population of Paris—men, women and children—fought for eight days after the entrance of the Versaillese, reflects as much the grandeur of their cause, as the infernal deeds of the soldiery reflect the innate spirit of that civilisation of which they are the mercenary vindicators. A glorious civilisation, indeed, the great problem of which is how to get rid of the heaps of corpses it made after the battle was over!

To find a parallel for the conduct of Thiers and his bloodhounds we must go back to the times of Sulla and the two Triumvirates of Rome. The same wholesale slaughter in cold blood; the same disregard, in massacre, of age and sex, the same system of torturing prisoners; the same proscriptions, but this time of a whole class; the same savage hunt after concealed leaders, lest one might escape; the same denunciations of political and private enemies; the same indifference for the butchery of entire strangers to the feud. There is but this difference, that the Romans had no *mitrailleuses* for the despatch, in the lump, of the proscribed, and that they had not "the law in their hands," nor on their lips the cry of "civilisation."

And after those horrors look upon the other still more hideous face of that bourgeois civilisation as described by its own press!

"With stray shots," writes the Paris correspondent of a London Tory paper, "still ringing in the distance, and untended wounded wretches dying amid the tombstones of Père la Chaise—with 6,000 terror-stricken insurgents wandering in an agony of despair in the labyrinth of the catacombs, and wretches hurried through the streets to be shot down in scores by the *mitrailleuse*—it is revolting to see the *cafés* filled with the votaries of absinthe, billiards and dominoes; female profligacy perambulating the boulevards, and the sound of revelry disturbing the night from the *cabinets particuliers* of fashionable restaurants."

M. Edouard Hervé writes in the *Journal de Paris,* a Versaillist journal pressed by the Commune:

"The way in which the population of Paris [!] manifested its satisfaction yesterday was rather more than frivolous, and we fear it will grow worse as time progresses. Paris has now a *fête* day appearance, which is sadly out of place; and, unless we are to be called the *Parisiens de la décadence,* this sort of thing must come to an end."

And then he quotes the passage from Tacitus:

"Yet, on the morrow of that horrible struggle, even before it was completely over, Rome—degraded and corrupt—began once more to wallow in the voluptuous slough which was destroying its body and polluting its soul—*alibi prœlia et vulnera, alibi balnea popinœque* [here fights and wounds, there baths and restaurants]."

M. Hervé only forgets to say that the "population of Paris" he speaks of is but the population of the Paris of M. Thiers—the *francs-fileurs* returning in throngs from Versailles, Saint-Denis, Rueil, and Saint Germain—*the* Paris of the "Decline."

In all its bloody triumphs over the self-sacrificing champions of a new and better society, that nefarious civilisation, based upon the enslavement of labour, drowns the moans of its victims in a hue-and-cry of calumny, reverberated by a world-wide echo. The serene working men's Paris of the Commune is suddenly changed into a pandemonium by the bloodhounds of "order." And what does this tremendous change prove to the bourgeois mind of all countries? Why, that the Commune has conspired against civilisation! The Paris people die enthusiastically for the Commune in numbers un-equalled in any battle known to history. What does that prove? Why, that the Commune was not the people's own government but the usurpation of a handful of criminals! The women of Paris joy-fully give up their lives at the barricades and on the place of execution. What does this prove? Why, that the demon of the Commune has changed them into Megæras and Hecates! The mod-eration of the Commune during two months of undisputed sway is equalled only by the heroism of its defence. What does that prove? Why, that for months the Commune carefully hid, under a mask of moderation and humanity, the bloodthirstiness of its fiend-ish instincts, to be let loose in the hour of its agony!

The working men's Paris, in the act of its heroic self-holocaust, involved in its flames buildings and monuments. While tearing to pieces the living body of the proletariat, its rulers must no longer expect to return triumphantly into the intact architecture of their abodes. The government of Versailles cries, "Incendiarism!" and whispers this cue to all its agents, down to the remotest hamlet, to hunt up its enemies everywhere as suspect of professional incendiarism. The bourgeoisie of the whole world, which looks complacently upon the wholesale massacre after the battle. is convulsed by horror at the desecration of brick and mortar!

When governments give state licences to their navies to "kill, *burn,* and destroy," is that a licence for incendiarism? When the British troops wantonly set fire to the Capitol at Washington and to the summer palace of the Chinese emperor, was that incendiarism? When the Prussians not for military reasons, but out of the mere spite of revenge, burned down, by the help of petroleum, towns like Chateâudun and innumerable villages, was that incendiarism? When Thiers, during six weeks, bombarded Paris, under the pretext that he wanted to set fire to those houses only in which there were people, was that incendiarism?—In war, fire is an arm as legitimate as any. Buildings held by the enemy are shelled to set them on fire. If their defenders have to retire, they themselves light the flames to prevent the attack from making use of the buildings. To be burned down has always been the inevitable fate of all buildings situated in the front of battle of all the regular armies of the world. But in the war of the enslaved against their enslavers, the only justifiable war in history, this is by no means to hold good! The Commune used fire strictly as a means of defence. They used it to stop up to the Versailles troops those long, straight avenues which Haussmann had expressly opened to artillery-fire; they used it to cover their retreat, in the same way as the Versaillese, in their advance, used their shells which destroyed at least as many buildings as the fire of the Commune. It is a matter of dispute, even now, which buildings were set fire to by the defence, and which by the attack. And the defence resorted to fire only then when the Versaillese troops had already commenced their wholesale murdering of prisoners.—Besides, the Com-

mune had, long before, given full public notice that if driven to
extremities, they would bury themselves under the ruins of Paris,
and make Paris a second Moscow, as the Government of Defence,
but only as a cloak for its treason, had promised to do. For this
purpose Trochu had found them the petroleum. The Commune
knew that its opponents cared nothing for the lives of the Paris
people, but cared much for their own Paris buildings. And Thiers,
on the other hand, had given them notice that he would be im-
placable in his vengeance. No sooner had he got his army ready
on one side, and the Prussians shutting up the trap on the other,
than he proclaimed: "I shall be pitiless! The expiation will be complete, and justice will be stern!" If the acts of the Paris working
men were vandalism, it was the vandalism of defence in despair,
not the vandalism of triumph, like that which the Christians per-
petrated upon the really priceless art treasures of heathen antiquity;
and even that vandalism has been justified by the historian as an
unavoidable and comparatively trifling concomitant to the titanic
struggle between a new society arising and an old one breaking
down. It was still less the vandalism of Haussmann, razing historic
Paris to make place for the Paris of the sightseer!

But the execution by the Commune of the sixty-four hostages,
with the Archbishop of Paris at their head! The bourgeoisie and
its army in June 1848 re-established a custom which had long disappeared from the practice of war—the shooting of their defenceless prisoners. This brutal custom has since been more or less
strictly adhered to by the suppressors of all popular commotions in
Europe and India; thus proving that it constitutes a real "progress
of civilisation"! On the other hand, the Prussians, in France, had
re-established the practice of taking hostages—innocent men, who,
with their lives, were to answer to them for the acts of others.
When Thiers, as we have seen, from the very beginning of the conflict, enforced the humane practice of shooting down the Communal
prisoners, the Commune, to protect their lives, was obliged to resort
to the Prussian practice of securing hostages. The lives of the hostages have been forfeited over and over again by the continued
shooting of prisoners on the part of the Versaillese. How could

they be spared any longer after the carnage with which Mac-Mahon's prætorians celebrated their entrance into Paris? Was even the last check upon the unscrupulous ferocity of bourgeois governments—the taking of hostages—to be made a mere sham of? The real murderer of Archbishop Darboy is Thiers. The Commune again and again had offered to exchange the archbishop, and ever so many priests in the bargain, against the single Blanqui, then in the hands of Thiers. Thiers obstinately refused. He knew that with Blanqui he would give to the Commune a head; while the archbishop would serve his purpose best in the shape of a corpse. Thiers acted upon the precedent of Cavaignac. How, in June 1848, did not Cavaignac and his men of order raise shouts of horror by stigmatising the insurgents as the assassins of Archbishop Affre! They knew perfectly well that the archbishop had been shot by the soldiers of order. M. Jacquemet, the archbishop's vicar-general, present on the spot, had immediately afterwards handed them in his evidence to that effect.

All this chorus of calumny, which the Party of Order never fail, in their orgies of blood, to raise against their victims, only proves that the bourgeois of our days considers himself the legitimate successor to the baron of old, who thought every weapon in his own hand fair against the plebeian, while in the hands of the plebeian a weapon of any kind constituted in itself a crime.

The conspiracy of the ruling class to break down the revolution by a civil war carried on under the patronage of the foreign invader—a conspiracy which we have traced from the very 4th of September down to the entrance of MacMahon's prætorians through the gate of St. Cloud—culminated in the carnage of Paris. Bismarck gloats over the ruins of Paris, in which he saw perhaps the first instalment of that general destruction of great cities he had prayed for when still a simple Rural in the Prussian *Chambre introuvable* of 1849. He gloats over the cadavres of the Paris proletariat. For him this is not only the extermination of revolution, but the extinction of France, now decapitated in reality, and by the French government itself. With the shallowness characteristic of all successful statesmen, he sees but the surface of this tremendous historic event. Whenever before has history exhibited the spectacle of a conqueror crowning his victory by turning into, not only the gendarme, but the hired bravo of the conquered government? There existed no war between Prussia and the Commune of Paris. On the contrary, the Commune had accepted the peace preliminaries, and Prussia had announced her neutrality. Prussia was, therefore, no belligerent. She acted the part of a bravo, a cowardly bravo, because incurring no danger; a hired bravo, because stipulating beforehand the payment of her blood-money of 500 millions on the fall of Paris. And thus, at last, came out the true character of the war, ordained by Providence as a chastisement of godless and debauched France by pious and moral Germany! And this unparalleled breach of the law of nations, even as understood by the old-world lawyers, instead of arousing the "civilised" governments of Europe to declare the felonious Prussian government, the mere tool of the St. Petersburg Cabinet, an outlaw amongst nations, only incites them to consider whether the few victims who escape the double cordon around Paris are not to be given up to the hangman of Versailles!

That after the most tremendous war of modern times, the conquering and the conquered hosts should fraternise for the common massacre of the proletariat—this unparalleled event does indicate, not, as Bismarck thinks, the final repression of a new society upheaving, but the crumbling into dust of bourgeois society. The highest heroic effort of which old society is still capable is national war; and this is now proved to be a mere governmental humbug, intended to defer the struggle of classes, and to be thrown aside as soon as that class struggle bursts out into civil war. Class rule is no longer able to disguise itself in a national uniform; the national governments are *one* as against the proletariat!

After Whit-Sunday, 1871, there can be neither peace nor truce possible between the working men of France and the appropriators of their produce. The iron hand of a mercenary soldiery may keep for a time both classes tied down in common oppression. But the battle must break out again and again in ever-growing dimensions, and there can be no doubt as to who will be the victor in the end— the appropriating few, or the immense working majority. And the

French working class is only the advanced guard of the modern proletariat.

While the European governments thus testify, before Paris, to the international character of class rule, they cry down the International Working Men's Association—the international counter-organisation of labour against the cosmopolitan conspiracy of capital —as the head fountain of all these disasters. Thiers denounced it as the despot of labour, pretending to be its liberator. Picard ordered that all communications between the French Internationals and those abroad should be cut off; Count Jaubert, Thiers' mummified accomplice of 1835, declares it the great problem of all civilised governments to weed it out. The Rurals roar against it, and the whole European press joins the chorus. An honourable French writer, completely foreign to our Association, speaks as follows:

"The members of the Central Committee of the National Guard, as well as the greater part of the members of the Commune, are the most active, intelligent, and energetic minds of the International Working Men's Association ... men who are thoroughly honest, sincere, intelligent, devoted, pure, and fanatical in the *good* sense of the word."

The police-tinged bourgeois mind naturally figures to itself the International Working Men's Association as acting in the manner of a secret conspiracy, its central body ordering, from time to time, explosions in different countries. Our Association is, in fact, nothing but the international bond between the most advanced working men in the various countries of the civilised world. Wherever, in whatever shape, and under whatever conditions the class struggle obtains any consistency, it is but natural that members of our Association should stand in the foreground. The soil out of which it grows is modern society itself. It cannot be stamped out by any amount of carnage. To stamp it out, the governments would have to stamp out the despotism of capital over labour—the condition of their own parasitical existence.

Working men's Paris, with its Commune, will be for ever celebrated as the glorious harbinger of a new society. Its martyrs are enshrined in the great heart of the working class. Its exterminators history has already nailed to that eternal pillory from which all the prayers of their priest will not avail to redeem them.

THE GENERAL COUNCIL

M. J. Boon, Fred. Bradnick, G. H. Buttery, Caihil, Delahaye, William Hales, A. Hermann, Kolb, Fred. Lessner, Lochner, T. P. Macdonnell, George Milner, Thomas Mottershead, Ch. Mills, Charles Murray, Pfander, Roach, Rochat, Ruhl, Sadler, A. Serraillier, Cowell Stepney, Alf. Taylor, William Townshend.

CORRESPONDING SECRETARIES

Eugene Dupont, *for France*

Karl Marx, *for Germany and Holland*

Fred. Engels, *for Belgium and Spain*

Hermann Jung, *for Switzerland*

P. Giovacchini, *for Italy*

Zevy Maurice, *for Hungary*

Anton Zabicki, *for Poland*

James Cohen, *for Denmark*

J. G. Eccarius, *for the United States*

Hermann Jung, *Chairman*

John Weston, *Treasurer*

George Harris, *Financial Secretary*

John Hales, *General Secretary*

Office: 256 High Holborn, London, W.C., *May 30, 1871*

Notes

"The column of prisoners halted in the Avenue Uhrich, and was drawn up, four or five deep, on the footway facing to the road. General Marquis de Gallifet and his staff dismounted and commenced an inspection from the left of the line. Walking down slowly and eyeing the ranks, the general stopped here and there, tapping a man on the shoulder or beckoning him out of the rear ranks. In most cases, without further parley, the individual thus selected was marched out into the centre of the road, where a small supplementary column was thus soon formed.... It was evident that there was considerable room for error. A mounted officer pointed out to General Gallifet a man and woman for some particular offence. The woman, rushing out of the ranks, threw herself on her knees, and, with outstretched arms, protested her innocence in passionate terms. The general waited for a pause, and then with most impassible face and unmoved demeanour, said: 'Madame, I have visited every theatre in Paris, your acting will have no effect on me' (*'ce n'est pas la peine de jouer la comedie'*).... It was not a good thing on that day to be noticeably taller, dirtier, cleaner, older, or uglier than one's neighbours. One individual in particular struck me as probably owing his speedy release from the ills of this world to his having a broken nose.... Over a hundred being thus chosen, a firing party told off, and the column resumed its march, leaving them behind. A few minutes afterwards a dropping fire in our rear commenced, and continued for over a quarter of an hour. It was the execution of the summarily-convicted wretches." —Paris Correspondent *Daily News*, June 8.—This Gallifet, "the kept man of his wife, so notorious for her shameless exhibitions at the orgies of the Second Empire," went, during the war, by the name of the French "Ensign Pistol."

"The *Temps*, which is a careful journal, and not given to sensation, tells a dreadful story of people imperfectly shot and buried before life was extinct. A great number were buried in the Square round St. Jacques-la-Bouchière; some of them very superficially. In the daytime the roar of the busy streets prevented any notice being taken; but in the stillness of the night the inhabitants of the houses in the neighbourhood were roused by distant moans, and in the morning a clenched hand was seen protruding through the soil. In consequence of this, exhumations were ordered to take place.... That many wounded have been buried alive I have not the slightest doubt. One case I can vouch for. When Brunel was shot with his mistress on the 24th ult. in the courtyard of a house in the Place Vendôme, the bodies lay there until the afternoon of the 27th. When the burial party came to remove the corpses, they found the woman living still, and took her to an ambulance. Though she had received four bullets she is now out of danger."—Paris Correspondent *Evening Standard,* June 8.

LETTERS TO DR. KUGELMANN ON THE
PARIS COMMUNE [67]

April 12, 1871

...If you look at the last chapter of my *Eighteenth Brumaire* you will find that I say that the next attempt of the French revolution will be no longer, as before, to transfer the bureaucratic-military machine from one hand to another, but to *smash* it, and this is essential for every real people's revolution on the Continent.[68] And this is what our heroic Party comrades in Paris are attempting. What elasticity, what historical initiative, what a capacity for sacrifice in these Parisians! After six months of hunger and ruin, caused rather by internal treachery than by the external enemy, they rise, beneath Prussian bayonets, as if there had never been a war between France and Germany and the enemy were not at the gates of Paris. History has no like example of a like greatness. If they are defeated only their "good nature" will be to blame. They should have marched at once on Versailles, after first Vinoy and then the reactionary section of the Paris National Guard had themselves retreated. The right moment was missed because of conscientious scruples. They did not want to *start the civil war,* as if that mischievous *abortion* Thiers had not already started the civil war with his attempt to disarm Paris. Second mistake: The Central Committee surrendered its power too soon, to make way for the Commune. Again from a too "honourable" scrupulosity! [69] However that may be, the present rising in Paris—even if it be crushed by the wolves, swine and vile curs of the old society—is the most glorious deed of our Party since the June insurrection in Paris. Compare these Parisians, storming heaven, with the slaves to heaven of the German-Prussian Holy Roman Empire, with its posthumous masquerades reeking of the barracks, the Church, cabbage-*junkerdom* and above all, of the philistine.

85

A propos. In the *official publication* of the list of those receiving direct subsidies from Louis Bonaparte's treasury there is a note that Vogt received 40,000 francs in August 1859. I have informed Liebknecht of the *fait*, for further use.

[London] April 17, 1871

...How you can compare petty-bourgeois demonstrations *à la* 13 June, 1849,[70] etc., with the present struggle in Paris is quite incomprehensible to me.

World history would indeed be very easy to make, if the struggle were taken up only on condition of infallibly favourable chances. It would, on the other hand, be of a very mystical nature, if "accidents" played no part. These accidents themselves fall naturally into the general course of development and are compensated again by other accidents. But acceleration and delay are very dependent upon such "accidents," which include the "accident" of the character of those who at first stand at the head of the movement.

The decisive, unfavourable "accident" this time is by no means to be found in the general conditions of French society, but in the presence of the Prussians in France and their position right before Paris. Of this the Parisians were well aware. But of this, the bourgeois *canaille* of Versailles were also well aware. Precisely for that reason they presented the Parisians with the alternative of taking up the fight or succumbing without a struggle. In the latter case, the demoralisation of the working class would have been a far greater misfortune than the fall of any number of "leaders." The struggle of the working class against the capitalist class and its state has entered upon a new phase with the struggle in Paris. Whatever the immediate results may be, a new point of departure of world-historic importance has been gained.

EXPLANATORY NOTES

[1] The wars (1813-14) of the German states, led by Prussia in alliance with the tsardom, against Napoleon I who annexed part of German territory to France and made the remainder subordinate to him.

[2] A quotation from the second Address of the General Council on the Franco-Prussian War. Marx foresaw that after the annexation of Alsace-Lorraine, France would be thirsting for revenge and would seek allies, turning in the first place, to tsarist Russia. On September 1, 1870, Marx wrote to Sorge:

"What the Prussian fools do not see is that the present war is leading just as inevitably to a war between Germany and Russia as the war of 1866 led to the war between Prussia and France. That is the *best result* I expect from it for Germany. Typical 'Prussianism' never has had and never can have any existence except in alliance with and subjection to Russia. And a war No. 2 of this kind will act as the midwife to the inevitable social revolution in Russia."

[3] The monarchists in France were at that time divided into three parties: the Legitimists—adherents of the "legitimate" dynasty of the Bourbons; the Orleanists—adherents of the Orleans dynasty; and the Bonapartists—adherents of Louis Bonaparte.

[4] The *coup d'état* of Louis Bonaparte by which he made himself Emperor. See Marx, *The Eighteenth Brumaire of Louis Bonaparte*. International Publishers, New York.

[5] The Second Empire in France was the name given to the period of the rule of Louis Bonaparte (Napoleon III, 1852-70) in distinction to the First Empire of Napoleon I (1804-14).

[6] The war with Austria was contrived by Bismarck in order to get rid of Prussia's old competitor in the unification of Germany. Prussia conquered Austria in this war and so secured the hegemony in German unification. Napoleon III remained neutral in the Austro-Prussian War because he hoped to receive as a reward part of the territory of the German states, as promised him by Bismarck.

[7] At Sedan (a town in northeast France) on September 2, 1870, the bulk of the French army, headed by the emperor, surrendered to the German troops.

[8] The mobile National Guard—reserve troops created by Napoleon III in 1868 for protection of the towns in case of war.

[9] For the purpose of municipal administration, Paris was divided into *arrondissements* each of which had a mayor at the head.

[10] Louis XVI was executed during the first French bourgeois revolution (on January 21, 1793).

[11] The split in the French Workers' Party, into the supporters of Brousse (Possibilists), and the supporters of Guesde (Marxists), took place at the congress in Etienne in 1882. The opportunist wing, the Possibilists or Broussists, who were hunting for electoral victories, repudiated the party programme, restricting themselves in their agitation solely to "realisable"

demands; they fought against party discipline, demanding autonomy for the local organisations in the question of the election platform and in the tactic of blocs with other parties.

[12] The Republican and Democratic Parties. At an earlier period the Democratic Party represented the interests of the landowning South, while the Republican Party represented the interests of the industrial North. Both parties are now representatives of finance capital.

[13] In all editions published previous to 1932 the text had the words "the German philistine." This was a falsification. Engels' manuscript, in the possession of the Marx-Engels-Lenin Institute in Moscow, has the words "the Social-Democratic philistine." The word "Social-Democratic" was afterwards crossed out (not by Engels) and the word "German" inserted in an unknown handwriting.

[14] The plebiscite was arranged by Napoleon III in order to consolidate his empire and undermine republican agitation in the country. On May 8, 1870, the nation was to express its attitude to certain of the government's liberal reforms and amendments introduced into the constitution. There voted, for the new constitution, and consequently for the empire, 7,358,786 persons, against 1,571,939, while 1,894,681 abstained from voting.

[15] This refers to the third court prosecution against the International taking place under the empire.

[16] The war between France and Germany began on July 19, 1870.

[17] See Karl Marx, *Selected Works*, Vol. II, p. 369. (International Publishers, New York.)

[18] On the German side, the war was a war of defence in so far as it was directed against Bonapartist France, which was interested in the dismemberment of Germany and hindered German unification (national unity was a basic question for the German bourgeois revolution). While giving this characterisation of the war, Marx and Engels at the same time demanded from the German Workers' Party that it should: (1) sharply distinguish between German national and Prussian dynastic interests; (2) oppose the annexation of Alsace-Lorraine; (3) make peace as soon as a republican, non-chauvinist government came to power in Paris; (4) unceasingly emphasise the unity of German and French workers, who did not approve of the war and had no quarrel with one another.

[19] The battle at Sadowa (in Bohemia) on July 3, 1866, played a decisive role in the Austro-Prussian war. After the Prussian victory over Austria, the latter was excluded from the German Federation and an important part of Bismarck's plan for the unification of Germany was accomplished (the creation of the North German Confederation).

[20] On the French side, the war was a dynastic one; Louis Bonaparte hoped by victory over the foreign foe to be able to save the crumbling edifice of the Bonapartist Empire.

[21] Germany conducted the war against Napoleon I in alliance with tsarist

Russia. By means of the "Holy Alliance," created after the victory over Napoleon I (1814-15), Russia attained a tremendous influence in international politics and began to play the role of "the gendarme of Europe." Prussia, as Marx expressed it, became "the fifth wheel of the coach of the European states."

22 The French army was heavily defeated at Sedan on September 2 and the emperor taken prisoner. On September 4, the republic was proclaimed in France and the so-called "Government of National Defence" set up.

23 By the Treaty of Tilsit (1807) France compelled Prussia to reduce the army, to pay a war indemnity of 100 million talers and to surrender territory in the west and east.

24 In 1865, Louis Bonaparte promised Bismarck France's neutrality in case of an Austro-Prussian war. In 1870, the Russian Foreign Minister Gorchakov promised Russia's neutrality in a Franco-Prussian war.

25 The Russian press attacked the Russian government for its friendly attitude toward Prussia.

26 The basis for this manifesto was Marx's letter of instructions to the committee of the German Social-Democratic Party (published in the *Volksstaat*, September 11, 1871).

27 In regard to this, Lenin wrote as follows, in his Preface to the Russian translation of Marx's *Letters to Kugelmann:*

"In September 1870, six months before the Commune, Marx emphatically warned the French workers, any attempt at upsetting the new government would be desperate folly, he said in his well-known Address of the International. He revealed *in advance* the nationalistic illusions concerning the possibility of a movement in the spirit of 1792. ...

"But when the *masses* rose Marx wanted to march with them, to learn with them in the process of the struggle and not to give them bureaucratic admonitions. He realised that it would be quackery or hopeless pedantry to attempt to calculate the chances in advance *with complete accuracy. Above everything else* he put the fact that the working class heroically, self-sacrificingly and taking the initiative itself, *makes* world history. Marx looked upon this history from the point of view of those who *make* it without being able to calculate *exactly* the chances beforehand and not from the point of view of a moralising intellectual and philistine who says: 'It was easy to foresee ... they should not have resorted to. ...'

"Marx was able to appreciate the fact that moments occurred in history when the desperate struggle of the *masses* even for a hopeless cause is *necessary* for the sake of the further education of these masses and their training for the *next* struggle." (International Publishers, New York, pp. 15-19.)

28 Marx has in mind the wave of national feeling among the masses in France in 1792 during the struggle with the attacking armies of the coalition of European states. He warns against a mechanical application of the slogan

"the fatherland in danger" to the Franco-Prussian war. "To fight the Prussians on behalf of the bourgeoisie would be madness." (Engels.)

[29] At the presidential election (December 10, 1848) Louis Bonaparte exploited the prejudices of the French peasants; they gave him their votes in recollection of Napoleon Bonaparte with whose name they erroneously associated the achievements of the first French bourgeois revolution.

[30] Marx has in mind the great campaign of meetings, which developed in England on the initiative of Marx and the General Council of the International, for securing recognition of the French republic.

[31] The war conducted by the first coalition of the powers (Austria, Prussia, Sardinia, etc.) against the first French bourgeois revolution. In February 1793, England and Holland, and in March Spain, also joined in the war.

[32] During the Civil War in America (1861-65) between the industrial North and the South, which upheld the system of slave plantations, the English bourgeoisie supported the South, i.e., slavery. This was due to the fact that the English bourgeoisie saw a growing rival in the industrial North, while the South represented a supplier of cotton for the English market.

[33] The ferocious suppression in Paris in 1839 of the rising of the Society for the Rights of Man during which unarmed persons, including women and children, were slaughtered.

[34] Ferdinand II of Naples was given the nickname of King Bomba on account of a furious bombardment of the town of Messina, September, 1848.

[35] This refers to the suppression of the June insurrection of the Paris proletariat in 1848.

[36] Don Carlos (1545-68). Spanish prince who took part in the conspiracy against his father. He is idealised by Schiller in the latter's tragedy, *Don Carlos*.

[37] The chief historical works of Thiers are: *History of the French Revolution* and *History of the Consulate and the Empire*.

[38] The French system of protection was marked by high import duties on commodities (*e.g.,* the duty on English cast-iron was 70 per cent of its value, that on iron 105 per cent of its value). As a result, many tools and other commodities which could not be produced in France vanished altogether from the market.

[39] The Chamber of Deputies in France which consisted mainly of extreme monarchists, representatives of the nobility, and was marked by its reactionary character.

[40] The National Assembly which opened in Bordeaux on February 13 had a majority of outspoken royalists (450 out of 750 deputies), chiefly representatives of the landowners. Hence its name of Assembly of "Rurals."

[41] Cayenne, capital of French Guiana in South America, notorious penal settlement.

[42] His function was to serve imprisonment if the newspaper was prosecuted.

[43] On October 31, 1870, an attempt was made to overthrow the Government of National Defence and to seize power. The impulse for the movement was provided by rumours of an armistice about to be concluded with the Prussians, of the defeat of the National Guard at Le Bourget (October 30) and of the capitulation of Metz. Led by Blanquists, a battalion of National Guards composed chiefly of workers, occupied the Town Hall, proclaimed the overthrow of the old government and the establishment of a new one which would organise elections to the Commune. The new government, which did not base itself on the masses, proved irresolute and vacillating. It entered into negotiations with the arrested members of the Government of National Defence and obtained from them a verbal promise to institute elections for the Commune (on November 1) and to declare a general amnesty. In the meantime battalions of the Civil Guard were concentrated at the Town Hall and on the morning of November 1, they occupied it and restored the Government of National Defence to power.

[44] On January 22, 1871, a new attempt was made to overthrow the Government of National Defence. The immediate occasion for this attempt was the defeat of the National Guard at Bougainville (January 19, 1871), rumours of an armistice and the appointment of General Vinoy as military governor of Paris. The attempt of January 22, exactly like that of October 31, was marked by lack of determination and unity, and absence of organisational contact with the masses. During its suppression, thirty persons were killed or wounded, including women and children.

[45] About these fatal mistakes of the Central Committee, Marx wrote to Kugelmann on April 12, 1871. See *Letters to Kugelmann*, p. 123, International Publishers, New York.

[46] Marx here formulates one of the fundamental lessons of the Paris Commune. The tremendous significance attached by Marx and Engels to this lesson is evident from their remarks in the Preface to *The Communist Manifesto*, dated June 24, 1872. There it is said that the Programme of *The Communist Manifesto* has "in some details become antiquated. One thing especially," they continue, "was proved by the Commune, *viz.*, that 'the working class cannot simply lay hold of the ready-made state machinery and wield it for its own purposes.' ..."

In this connection, Lenin wrote:

"It is extremely characteristic that it is precisely this vital correction that has been distorted by the opportunists, and its meaning, probably, is not known to nine-tenths, if not ninety-nine hundredths, of the readers of *The Communist Manifesto* ... The current vulgar 'interpretation' of Marx's famous utterance quoted above is that Marx here emphasises the idea of gradual development in contradistinction to the seizure of power, and so on.

"As a matter of fact, *exactly the opposite is the case.* Marx's idea is that the working class must *break up, smash* the 'ready-made state machinery,' and not confine itself merely to laying hold of it.

"On April 12, 1871, *i.e.*, just at the time of the Commune, Marx wrote to Kugelmann:

" 'If you look at the last chapter of my *Eighteenth Brumaire,* you will find that I say that the next attempt of the French Revolution will be no longer, as before, to transfer the bureaucratic-military machine from one hand to the other, but to *smash* it (Marx's italics—the original is *zerbrechen*); and this is essential for every real people's revolution on the Continent. And this is what our heroic Party comrades in Paris are attempting.' (*Die Neue Zeit,* XX, I, 1901-02, p. 709. The letters of Marx to Kugelmann have come out in Russian in no less than two editions, one of them edited and with an introduction by me.)

"The words, 'to smash' 'the bureaucratic-military state machinery,' briefly express the principal lesson of Marxism on the tasks of the proletariat in relation to the state during a revolution. And it is precisely this lesson that has been not only completely forgotten, but positively distorted, in the prevailing Kautskyan 'interpretation' of Marxism." (V. I. Lenin, *Selected Works,* Vol. VII, pp. 36-37. International Publishers, New York.)

[47] The wars waged by England, Russia, Prussia, Austria, Spain and other states against revolutionary France and later against the empire of Napoleon I.

[48] Refers to the Bonapartist empire.

[49] In connection with this characterisation of the Commune as a new type of state, Lenin wrote:

" 'A working, not a parliamentary body'—this hits the nail on the head in regard to the present-day parliamentarians and the parliamentary 'lap dogs' of Social-Democracy! Take any parliamentary country, from America to Switzerland, from France to England, Norway and so forth—in these countries the actual work of the 'state' is done behind the scenes and is carried on by the departments, the government offices and the General Staffs. Parliament itself is given up to talk for the special purpose of fooling the 'common people.'..."

"The Commune was to have substituted for the venal and rotten parliamentarism of bourgeois society institutions in which freedom of opinion and discussion would not have degenerated into deception, for the parliamentarians would have had to work themselves, would have had to execute their own laws, they themselves would have had to test their results in real life; they would have been directly responsible to their constituents. Representative institutions would have remained, but there was to have been *no* parliamentarism as a special system, as the division of labour between the legislative and the executive, as a privileged position for deputies...."

"There can be no thought of destroying officialdom immediately everywhere, completely. That is utopia. But to *smash* the old bureaucratic machine at once and to begin immediately to construct a new one that will enable all officialdom to be gradually abolished is *not* utopia, it is the experience of the Commune, it is the direct and immediate task of the revolutionary proletariat." (*Ibid.*, pp. 44-47.)

[50] In regard to this characterisation of parliamentarism, Lenin wrote:

"Thanks to the prevalence of social-chauvinism and opportunism, this remarkable criticism of parliamentarism made in 1871 also belongs now to the 'forgotten words' of Marxism...

"To decide once every few years which member of the ruling class is to misrepresent the people in parliament is the real essence of bourgeois parliamentarism, not only in parliamentary-constitutional monarchies, but also in the most democratic republics." (*Ibid.*, pp. 43-44.)

[51] The Girondins were the party of the industrial and trading bourgeoisie during the epoch of the first French bourgeois revolution. Wishing to behead the revolution and to weaken the centralisation of revolutionary forces, they endeavoured to convert France into a Federation and to destroy the leading role of revolutionary Paris.

[52] Analysing the tremendous historical importance of the lessons derived by Marx from the experience of the Paris Commune, Lenin wrote:

"The utopians busied themselves with 'inventing' the political forms under which the socialist transformation of society was to take place. The anarchists waived the question of political forms altogether. The opportunists of present-day Social-Democracy accepted the bourgeois political forms of the parliamentary democratic state as the unsurpassable limit; they battered their foreheads praying before this idol and denounced every attempt to *smash* these forms as anarchism.

"Marx deduced from the whole history of Socialism and of the political struggle that the state was bound to disappear, and that the transitional form of its disappearance (the transition from state to no state) would be the 'proletariat organised as the ruling class.' But Marx did not set out to discover the political *forms* of this future stage. He limited himself to a precise observation of French history, to analysing it, and to the conclusion to which the year 1851 had led, *viz.,* that matters were moving towards the *smashing* of the bourgeois state machine.

"And when the mass revolutionary movement of the proletariat burst forth, Marx, in spite of the failure of that movement, in spite of its short life and its patent weakness, began to study the political forms that it had *disclosed.*

"The Commune is the form 'at last discovered' by the proletarian revolution, under which to work out the economic emancipation of labour.

"The Commune is the first attempt of a proletarian revolution to *smash* the bourgeois state machine and it constitutes the political form, 'at last discovered,' which can and must *supersede* the smashed machine.

"We shall see below that the Russian Revolutions of 1905 and 1917, in different circumstances and under different conditions, continued the work

of the Commune and corroborated Marx's brilliant historical analysis."
(*Ibid.*, p. 53.)

[53] The Central Committee of the National Guard as late as March 20 had postponed payment on bills of exchange until October 1, 1871. On April 18, the Commune promulgated a decree postponing payments on debt obligations for three years.

[54] Free-thinking, hostile to the priests and the church.

[55] The Bourbon dynasty, which was restored to power after the overthrow of Napoleon I, decided to compensate the French nobility for the land taken from it during the first French bourgeois revolution. One milliard francs was paid to the nobility.

[56] The 45 centime tax was introduced in 1848 by the bourgeois provisional government with the object of creating dissension between the proletariat and the peasantry. The government gave as the reason for the tax the necessity of feeding the workers. The increase of taxation on the peasants by almost 50 per cent turned the peasantry against the revolution and the republic.

[57] The Party of Order during the 1848 Revolution united the royalist big bourgeoisie and the landowners.

[58] Alsace and Lorraine.

[59] During the Second Empire, Baron Haussmann was Prefect of the Department of the Seine, *i.e.*, of the City of Paris. He caused a number of new streets and buildings to be constructed.

[60] In the church of St. Laurent were discovered skeletons of women who had been violated by the monks and buried alive in the vaults. In the Picpus nunnery women were held on the pretext that they were insane, and they suffered the same fate.

[61] Irish landlords who squandered their "income" outside the country, hardly ever visiting their estates.

[62] The tennis court where in 1789 the National Assembly took an oath not to dissolve, in spite of the royal command, before the constitution had been drafted.

[63] The centre of the counter-revolutionary nobility in emigration during the first French bourgeois revolution.

[64] De Calonne was Comptroller General (a kind of Prime Minister) in France on the eve of the 1789 Revolution.

[65] The outbreak of the revolution and proclamation of the Commune in Lyons occurred on March 22, and in Marseilles on March 23; both were quickly crushed by the Thiers government. The Commune was also proclaimed in Toulouse, Narbonne, St. Etienne and some other towns.

[66] By the commercial treaty with England concluded by Napoleon III in 1860, duties on English goods were lowered.

[67] In the letters to Kugelmann published here, Marx gives an estimate of the Paris Commune and characterises it as a "historic experiment of gigantic

importance, as an advance of the world proletarian revolution, as a practical step that was more important than hundreds of programmes and discussions." (*Ibid.,* p. 35.)

Concerning Marx's letter of April 12, Lenin wrote in 1907 that it was "a letter which we would gladly see hung on the wall of the home of every Russian Social-Democrat and of every literate Russian worker." (V. I. Lenin, Preface to Karl Marx's *Letters to Kugelmann,* p. 18.)

In this letter to Kugelmann, Marx formulates, as Lenin says, "more accurately, more clearly and better" those extraordinarily important conclusions for the Marxist theory of the state which he had arrived at on the basis of the world-historic experience of the Commune.

"It is clear that Marx's April letter (April 12, 1871) expresses the *same* thought that is contained in the Address of the General Council of the International written in the end of May (dated May 30, 1871).

"That which in *The Civil War* is called 'the ready-made state machine' is called in the letter of April 12, 1871, 'the bureaucratic-military machine'; that which in *The Civil War* is expressed by the words 'simply lay hold of,' is in the letter of April 12, 1871, once again formulated more exactly, clearly and better: 'to transfer ... from one hand to another.' And the addition, which does not exist in *The Civil War,* is especially striking: not to transfer the ready-made [machine] from one hand to another, but to *smash* it. And this the Commune *began* to do, but unfortunately did not carry it to completion." (V. I. Lenin, *Marxism on the State.*)

Lenin emphasises Marx's high estimate of the historical initiative of the masses in the letter to Kugelmann of April 17. Lenin contrasts this estimate of Marx with the estimates of the Revolution of 1905 by the Russian Mensheviks. He points out the great gulf in regard to this question between Marx and Plekhanov, who after the defeat of the Revolution of 1905 arrived at the cowardly opportunist conclusion that "they should not have resorted to arms."

"The homage paid to the *historical initiative* of the masses by this profound thinker who foresaw failure six months ahead—and the lifeless, soulless pedantic: 'They should not have resorted to arms!' Are these not as far apart as heaven is from earth. ...

"... Marx was able to appreciate the fact that moments occurred in history when the desperate struggle of the *masses* even for a hopeless cause is *necessary* for the sake of the further education of these masses and their training for the *next struggle.*" (V. I. Lenin, Preface to Marx's *Letters to Kugelmann,* pp. 16, 19.)

And just as Marx drew extremely important lessons from the experience of the defeated Paris Commune for his teachings on the state, so the even more significant world-historic experience of the successful proletariat of the Soviet Union, provided, at the hands of Lenin, and Stalin, extremely rich material for further development of Marx's teachings on the revolution, on the state and on the dictatorship of the proletariat.

[68] In *State and Revolution* Lenin explained as follows why Marx restricted his conclusions to the Continent:

"This was natural in 1871, when England was still the model of a purely capitalist country, but without militarism and, to a considerable degree, without a bureaucracy. Hence, Marx excluded England, where a revolution, even a people's revolution, could be conceived of, and was then possible, *without* the condition of first destroying the 'ready-made state machine.'

"Today, in 1917, in the epoch of the first great imperialist war, Marx's exception is no longer valid. Both England and America, the greatest and last representatives of Anglo-Saxon 'liberty,' in the sense that militarism and bureaucracy are absent, have today plunged headlong into the all-European, filthy, bloody morass of bureaucratic-military institutions to which everything is subordinated and which trample everything under foot. Today, both in England and America, the 'essential' thing for 'every real people's revolution' is the *smashing,* the *destruction* of the 'ready-made state machine' (brought in those countries, between 1914 and 1917, to general 'European' imperialist perfection)."

Further, Lenin emphasises that Marx makes use of the concept of "people's revolution" and explains this concept as follows:

"In Europe, in 1871, there was not a single country on the Continent in which the proletariat constituted the majority of the people. A 'people's' revolution, that swept actually the majority into its stream, could be such only if it embraced the proletariat and the peasantry. Both classes then constituted the 'people.' Both classes were united by the fact that the 'bureaucratic-military state machine' oppressed, crushed, exploited them. To *smash* this machine, to *break it up*—this is what is truly in the interests of the 'people,' of the majority, the workers and most of the peasants, this is what is 'essential' for the free alliance between the poor peasantry and the proletarians; without such an alliance democracy is unstable and the socialist reformation is impossible.

"As is well known, the Paris Commune strove for such an alliance, although it failed to achieve it owing to a number of circumstances, internal and external." (V. I. Lenin, *Selected Works,* Vol. VII, pp. 37-38.)

[69] In his notes on the letters of Marx to Kugelmann, Lenin summarises the essence of the mistakes of the Commune and the historical merits of the Communards in the following words:

"Both mistakes consist in the lack of offensive, in the lack of consciousness and determination to *smash* the state bureaucratic-military machine and the power of the bourgeoisie. What aroused Marx's enthusiasm in the Paris Commune? *The flexibility, the historical initiative, the capacity for self-sacrifice* among these Parisians, 'The Parisians storming heaven.'" (V. I. Lenin, *Marxism on the State.*)

[70] See Marx, *The Class Struggles in France,* 1848-50, Chap. III. International Publishers, New York.